Dear Nurse Me...

Reflections

*An anthology of letters
from six nurses*

Compiled by
Wendy Trevarthen

First published by Ultimate World Publishing 2022
Copyright © 2022 Wendy Trevarthen

ISBN

Paperback: 978-1-922714-61-9
Ebook: 978-1-922714-62-6

Wendy Trevarthen has asserted her rights under the Copyright, Designs and Patents Act 1988 to be identified as the author of this work. The information in this book is based on the author's experiences and opinions. The publisher specifically disclaims responsibility for any adverse consequences which may result from use of the information contained herein. Permission to use information has been sought by the author. Any breaches will be rectified in further editions of the book.

All rights reserved. No part of this publication may be reproduced, stored in or introduced into a retrieval system, or transmitted in any form, or by any means (electronic, mechanical, photocopying, recording or otherwise) without the prior written permission of the author. Any person who does any unauthorised act in relation to this publication may be liable to criminal prosecution and civil claims for damages. Enquiries should be made through the publisher.

Cover design: Ultimate World Publishing
Layout and typesetting: Ultimate World Publishing
Editor: Isabelle Russell
Cover photo license: Andrei_Barbulescu1-Shutterstock.com

Ultimate World Publishing
Diamond Creek,
Victoria Australia 3089
www.writeabook.com.au

Legal Disclaimer:

This book is designed to inform and motivate our readers. The content of each chapter is the sole expression and opinion of its author. The individual author(s) shall be liable for any physical, psychological, emotional, financial or commercial damages, including, but not limited to, special, incidental, consequential of other damages. Our views and rights are the same: You are responsible for your own choices, actions and results.

Authors have tried to recreate events, locales and conversations from their memories of them. To maintain their anonymity in some instances, authors have changed the names of individuals and places, and may have changed some identifying characteristics and details such as physical properties, occupations and places of residence.

Dedication

Dedicated to our mentoring nurses who have journeyed with us, paving our way forward.

Contents

Dedication	v
Acknowledgement of Country	1
Preface	3
Chapter 1: Anchor Points *John Rosenberg*	7
Chapter 2: Dare to Aspire *Judy Lonergan*	37
Chapter 3: A Passionate Purpose *Wendy Trevarthen*	65
Chapter 4: Finding Your Niche *Desley Joyce*	95
Chapter 5: Fighting for a Calling *Kris Murphy*	121
Chapter 6: To Be a Nurse *Jackie Morgan*	157
Afterward *Judy Lonergan, Wendy Trevarthen*	177
References	183

Acknowledgement of Country

We acknowledge the Traditional Owners and Custodians of this land, who have walked and cared for this land for thousands of years, and their descendants who maintain their spiritual connection and traditions.

We thank them for sharing their cultures, spiritualities and ways of living with the land in this place we all now call home.

We pay respect to Elders past, present and emerging.

May we continue to walk gently and respectfully with each other.

Preface

Nurses are not made, they are born. Born out of DNA that makes up the core essentials of being a nurse. Once a nurse, always a nurse. It's hard to shake this identity, and I question who would want to when they are born to nurse.

Nurses work all over the world; they form the glue in every healthcare system. They cry, they laugh, they can be frustrated, they can be elated. They are human.

It is this humanity that I called upon to magnetise this group of six nurses to share our stories so far, and to impart words of wisdom to those who are thinking about nursing as a profession, who have just started their journey, those who are amongst it, and for those that look back on their profession with pride.

I have had the idea behind this book for about four years and asked a few nurses that I have journeyed with, to join me on this adventure. What I found in collating our contributions to this book was that the journey for us all provided a creative outlet to write, (in a safe space) some stories that had played on our minds for some time.

We learn in our training about 'reflective practice' and indeed we all support this as a learning activity that leads us to becoming more proficient learners and practitioners. This project took the 'rules' off this and allowed each author to talk openly about their true feelings and the impact this has had on their expression of their authentic selves.

Nursing education, as we all know, has undergone a huge transformation over our lifetimes. All of these authors trained during a time when we were apprentices of our profession, supplying our employing hospitals with an eager on-the-job workforce.

We have evolved as the profession transitioned into the higher education sector and beyond, through many reforms and reviews. This must have an impact on our views of our profession, and our self-perception of where we are now. This is reflected in this book and presented in ways in which we hope will resource our younger nurses with some strategies to aspire to.

We pull no punches here; we are raw and authentic. We need to be because nursing is raw and real. We deal with things that no-one else does. We don't walk away, and if we do, it is for very good reasons. We are always there for our patients.

Nursing has been the foundation of many other professions – we were performing physiotherapy before physiotherapy was invented (Sister Kenny), we invented infection control, quality measures, management and education before they were based on a science (Florence Nightingale) and we have saved so many lives along the way. I'm not just talking about the patients we look after, but our family, our communities and our colleagues.

It truly is a profession at the heart of humanity.

Wendy Trevarthen

CHAPTER 1

Anchor Points

John Rosenberg

Dedication:

This chapter is dedicated to my nephew and godson, Luke Daniel Farrelly, born 25th October 1998, who died during the writing of this chapter on 25th July 2021. A remarkable young man, Luke's life was immeasurably enriched by his extraordinary parents and mighty brothers.

Hello John,

You're starting something that you're going to do for decades to come – nursing. You always thought you'd be a teacher and guess what? You do eventually become one, but teaching nurses. And others too, using some skills you'll hone over the years ahead. I've got so much more to tell you about that! And here you are at Wangaratta Hospital, doing your General Nursing training.

It was a bit of a left turn for you in Year 11 when Mr Downie asked you the question about nursing, but it's one that has turned out to be a game-changer for you. Hold your nerve – it's worth it. Nursing is something that you'll grow into. It doesn't exactly 'come naturally' to you. You have buckets of empathy and fertile ground for growing in compassion, but many of the practicalities take longer to soak in. I know how much curiosity you have for human physiology and passion for the experiences people go through when their time is running out. These will come in handy as you increasingly focus your career on palliative care. But more on that later.

The experience of witnessing firsthand your grandmother's sudden death will inform so many of your values and shape so many of your choices in your life. Being just 15 is an impressionable time and that experience certainly did make an impression on you. With time, the terrible shock will dissipate and the legacy of the experience will endure in life-changing ways. Hang in there. The compassion borne from it is fundamental to who you are becoming.

There's something coming near the end of your nursing training that also going to shake you for years. It's brief but malicious, and it poses an actual threat to your life. Obviously, you do survive without lasting physical injury. Unfortunately, there's no getting around it and you'll feel the psychological impact for much of your life. It'll open your eyes to the reality that some people are following paths that you were utterly oblivious to. But the good news is that, eventually, some friends you can trust will help you overcome the enduring trauma in an unexpected yet simple way.

Yes, you're going to carry some baggage in the years ahead (who doesn't?), but you are now, and will always be, a man driven by just a few core values: compassion, curiosity and connection. These will provide you with anchor points in your life and work. This letter serves to show you what they are and why they matter so much. I'm not going to tell you what to do (well, not much anyway). I'm going to let you know how they help you navigate your life as a nurse.

Compassion

Do you remember that time in primary school when you got upset because the new kid, Peter, was being bullied by the same kids who were bullying you? How sad you felt for him – funny name, funny-looking, couldn't run – and how powerless, how weak, you felt? I think the seeds of compassion were always there, but it takes years for you to understand that being compassionate is not at all about weakness or powerlessness. Quite the opposite, in fact. These 'soft' skills actually require strength and resilience. 'Steadfast' is a word that will emerge as the years go by.

What brought this compassion out in you? Of course, the first game-changer was Grandmother's death.

It was the August school holidays and I was 15. Grandmother had asked me to help her with moving some pot plants around her back veranda. She was a little woman, and I'd overtaken her in height by then. We were very close, and I loved to help her and Grandfather around their house.

Grandmother had been in and out of hospital, and I was to find out later that she had heart disease that was progressively worsening, and that she was neglecting the signs of her disease. She'd had an episode earlier in the day that I came to understand as one of chest pain, a precursor to what was to follow that afternoon.

As we were moving the pot plants around, I heard her say, 'Ooh, Johnny, quick!' As I turned, she fell back against the doorstep. I yelled for Grandfather and Uncle Murray as I held her, and they ran from the house to her, grabbing her and taking her inside. The disbelief at the sight of her lying on the kitchen floor, Grandfather and Uncle Murray doing CPR… the physicality, the force of it. The urgency of calling the doctor (no such thing as paramedics in those days), the knot in the guts while calling Mum, telling her,

Anchor Points

> 'It's really bad,' when what I wanted to say was, 'I think she's dead.' Then leaving the scene to wait for Mum to arrive on her bicycle.
>
> She'd died at that moment of collapse. Died in my arms.

You'll eventually be able to articulate how this creates the drive to make a career of palliative care. That not everyone gets to say what needs to be said, let alone say goodbye. You end up doing a PhD in palliative care, and your brief dedication to Grandmother cuts to the core of this drive in simple words.

> This work is dedicated to the memory of Evelyn Lucy Downing, 29 November 1909 – 27 August 1980, whose death taught me that time is precious and can make all the difference in the world.

Palliative care presents opportunities for finding those moments before death comes, and it's a place where compassion is central to supporting the individuals and families in your care. But it's tricky, sometimes. In the early days, you assume that resolution of family conflict, that reconciliation and words of love is what good dying is made of. In fact, you'll see a lot of people in palliative care trying to push families into 'resolution'. You come to see the reality that this isn't achieved (or even sought) by everyone. Many people die as they've lived, and your naivety eventually fades as you experience more and more families whose lives are far from calm and reconcilable.

> *Eric's family – wife, Barbara, and two daughters – were looking after him at home as his emphysema gradually worsened. They were struggling, all of them. Eric seemed very intolerant of his family's attempts to help yet they persisted. Eventually, his symptoms become unstable and he's admitted to the local palliative care unit for stabilisation, to return to his home in a week or so.*
>
> *I popped in on Barbara while Eric was in hospital to check on her and help her prepare for Eric's discharge from hospital. And that is when she tells me, 'There's no way that bastard is ever coming back to this house.' I still remember the exact words!*
>
> *It turns out that Eric was indeed a bastard. A cruel and violent man, he'd beaten Barbara countless times over the years, and on occasions would lock her and the girls outside of the house overnight in all types of weather. His lifelong rage had been suppressed by his illness, but the cruelty remained in his hold over his family.*

Anchor Points

> *Barbara explained that, to keep the peace, she'd cared for him for as long as he was able to stay at home, but the minute he went to hospital for inpatient care, that was it. She flat out refused to have him home. So, he was placed in a nursing home where he lived for a few more months before his death. He died as he'd lived – with a chasm of distance from the very people he could've had by his side in his living and dying. Resolution was never on the table.*

You've also just met Roxy, who'll become one of your closest lifelong friends. What is it about edge-dwellers that appeals to you so much? Is it because your strong sense of needing to belong also draws you to those renegades who push the boundaries? Roxy's personal story shocks you to the core. Your ignorance of the type of damage done in her early life is another formative experience as you come to understand how different the life experiences of others can be. Yet she is a strong, articulate, resilient and values-driven woman whose compassion lies with those way beyond the edges.

John, you'll soon see that compassion is not quite like some of the dreadful dictionary definitions you read about: '**compassion:** (*noun*) sympathetic pity and concern for the sufferings or misfortunes of others.'[i] Bloody hell. No wonder it sounds soft.

For a start, you'll learn that compassion is as much a verb as it is a noun. Yes, the recognition of the suffering of others and a heartfelt desire to alleviate it are the roots of compassion; but these are incomplete without action. In palliative care, these actions are both clinical and interpersonal. You'll learn the clinical exercise of compassion as you grow in your knowledge and skills in assessment, care planning, symptom management, psychological care, family support, teamwork and partnership and so much more.

The interpersonal nature of palliative care is fundamental to putting it into practice. You'll publish one of your earliest journal articles about this, 'Therapeutic relationships in specialist palliative care nursing practice.' [ii] Your co-authors figure large in your future – Deebs becomes one of your dearest friends and Patsy becomes your mentor, boss and PhD supervisor. Both are deep thinkers in quite different ways and their collaborations with you over the years stimulate, challenge and nurture your curiosity. But more on that later. The article shows that at the very centre of palliative care nursing practice is the therapeutic relationship. Its qualities are based in trust and alliance between the nurse and the patient and their carers; it's about *being with* not just *doing to*. There is no place for benign paternalism here – it demands a human interaction as the exercise of compassion. You'll bring expertise, alliance and trust to many of the people you care for over the years ahead. And when you get it wrong (and you will, despite your high expectations), it'll often be because you've forgotten this fundamental point.

Maybe this is why some of your nursing experiences stick fast in your memory, when you've seen the violation of this very quality?

> *Albert was a middle-aged man who'd come in from Mayday Hills, an 'asylum' in nearby Beechworth. A man with a significant intellectual disability, Albert was non-verbal. He'd had gastric surgery and had a wide-bore nasogastric tube in. The surgeon, intimidating in stature as well as demeanour, swept into the room with his entourage, surrounding Albert's bed. Albert looked terrified as the surgeon quickly untaped the tubing and, without pause, yanked the tube out at speed, flicking mucus across the room. Albert yelped, while the surgeon turned and marched onwards. An imperious cruelty.*

One lesson you'll learn in your life is that you, like most people, are made up of contradictions. The surgeon whose interaction hurt Albert also showed another patient an unexpected kindness.

> *Gary was about 37 and had come into hospital for abdominal surgery. His was an 'open and shut' case – advanced malignancy throughout his abdominal cavity. He returned to the ward, and the same surgeon who so roughly removed Albert's nasogastric tube, sat by Gary's bed and told him the bad news. I remember Gary's puzzled look – 'You mean it's cancer?' The surgeon gently told him again and that he had just six weeks to live but that he, Gary, would be kindly cared for there. The contrast was stark in his interaction with Gary and Albert.*

You'll show these contradictions yourself, of course. You're an impulsive bloke, and often careless in what you say. You're funny alright, but not always! Learn to keep a lid on the smart remarks – it's easy to offend others despite your benevolent intentions. These failures are also your lessons, and you'll grow as a result.

You're a young man with a strong faith, and this faith helps you grow in your understanding of compassion. Your spirituality evolves, as you'd expect, and you'll eventually find a description of compassion that captures all these different elements. The Charter for Compassion is introduced to you by a friend you'll meet in your fifties; Terry is a man whose understanding of compassion holds that balance between the noun and verb! With the

Golden Rule at its heart, compassion is about action and the humility of not being the most obvious or important one in our relationships with others:

> *'The principle of compassion lies at the heart of all religious, ethical and spiritual traditions, calling us always to treat all others as we wish to be treated ourselves. Compassion impels us to work tirelessly to alleviate the suffering of our fellow creatures, to dethrone ourselves from the centre of our world and put another there, and to honour the inviolable sanctity of every single human being, treating everybody, without exception, with absolute justice, equity and respect.'* [iii]

In your thirties, you hear about an approach to palliative care that gives form to a range of values, views and experiences in your work life. 'Health Promoting Palliative Care'[iv] is developed by an Australian sociologist, Allan Kellehear, which situates palliative care in its broader social context. The clinical care, the therapeutic relationship, the place of the patient and their family in broader social networks and communities, become the space where you begin to consolidate the broad understanding you have of your work and values. It's going to be one of your most exciting curiosities (remember the PhD I mentioned earlier? Just wait until I tell you about that!).

In time, 'Health Promoting Palliative Care' morphs into 'Public Health Palliative Care' and eventually you step up to lead an international association that promotes it.[v] This gives you many opportunities for international travel and this will continue to open your eyes to the endless expressions of compassion in so many different places. In palliative care, what compassion looks like in Canada is different to India, the UK or Ireland. Yet you'll see that in each of these places, the fundamentals of compassion are behind their local expressions.

You'll also be challenged to exercise compassion in your leadership role, as it brings encounters that you won't expect. More contradiction! It'll remind you that reconciliation isn't everyone's goal, but you're going to find a life motto, and the challenges of your leadership will be founded on it.

So, be strong, trust in compassion as a way to live your life and do your work in palliative care. You're idealistic now, and it won't leave you. This call to compassion is challenging and living it out in your life and work takes strength and persistence.

It is worth it. Without any doubt, it's better to try than not.

Connection

I suspect your distress over Peter's bullying was a projection of your own. Funny name (well, it was uncommon anyway), funny looking (that is, very short) and couldn't run? Sounds familiar. And other differences you've struggled with that make you feel on the outer with so many? You've been good at school, you love music and art, you're lousy at sport and, to be honest, a bit socially awkward. The overconfident, outgoing, smart-mouthed joker is also pretty scared and wonders where he belongs, right? Contradictions abound.

Yet this drive to promote and live in strong connection with others is one of your core values. You'll duck out of nursing for a couple of years after you graduate to join an intentional community – that faith of yours and the urge to live out a compassionate existence have you pursue a vocation of a different kind. It runs its course, and you return to nursing with greater clarity than before about what matters to you. It also brings you into the orbit of a compassionate and connected woman called Caren. You become friends over these shared values and you'll immediately admire her own commitment to living with and supporting children with disabilities in another intentional community. Then guess what? You end up marrying her and it will be a lifelong commitment that you'll hold dear. It's not always going to be easy, but its connection and compassion as individuals and as a couple that creates a worthwhile life together. Your sense of belonging in the life you'll make with Caren is one mighty anchor point.

Is it a surprise that you've joined a profession where your sense of belonging is both realised and challenged? A man in nursing at a time when it was still pretty uncommon? You belong to a profession, certainly, but by virtue of your gender, you will have to justify *how* and *why* you belong too.

> *I loved being a community nurse in Brisbane during my thirties. Two experiences stand out as direct confrontations of my place in nursing.*
>
> *The first was Derek, a single man in his forties who lived with his parents and brother in a rough suburb. Derek's mum, Mavis, was an elderly lady with dementia. Part of my job was to assist Mavis with showering and after a couple of weeks of visiting the family, Derek walked up to me and said, 'What type of job is this for a man?' I was taken aback, but before I could answer, he went on, 'You must be some kind of fuckin' pervert to shower old ladies for a living.' I stammered, 'Look, mate, I'm not your enemy here.' But he demanded I leave the house and not come back. I explained this to his father, and other arrangements were put in place for Mavis' care.*

I'd never been confronted so aggressively about being a male nurse, and haven't since.

Usually, the objections to my gender were more suppressed or snide. I was performing an admission assessment for a woman in the inner suburbs, and this took about an hour. It required a range of clinical knowledge and practice skills, as well as interpersonal skills and resource knowledge. It was Community Nursing 101, and I was good at it. At the end of the assessment visit, having designed a plan for care and arranged follow up services, the patient's husband accompanied me to the front gate and, farewelled me with the words, 'Next time, get them to send a real nurse.' I was shocked, then angry.

Statistically speaking, men in nursing are still pretty uncommon, so you'll remain in a minority group throughout your nursing career. But many colleagues – both women and men – will influence your sense of self and belonging in your chosen career.

Before that happens though, you're soon going to experience the real possibility of the ultimate disconnection from others – the prospect of your death. Being connected is everything to you. Where these connections are endangered, then your sense of self is endangered too. Your life is going to be put under real threat.

The ultimate violation of my sense of connection – present and possible – came with being caught up in an armed robbery at the hospital late in my third year of nursing training. Back in the 1980s, our regional hospital wasn't lockable, and we had a single security guard on duty at night. We had had a number of robberies of the drug safes during my time there, and I'd been caught up in one brief one early on, but this one was a cracker.

Night duty, almost midnight, and time for me to head down to the cafeteria for the night meal. Walking down past the side corridor from the kitchens, a figure steps out from behind the plastic doors, head covered and two pistols at my face. I can still feel that moment when my blood drained from my face. 'Oh yeah, OK,' I said (I think I even did an eye roll). Moments later, we arrived at the reception – I remember the receptionist looking quizzically at the perpetrator, then at me and her face fell. We were wordlessly pointed (with pistols) up the stairs and around to the surgical ward where the biggest batch of injectable narcotics would be. Forced to the floor, about four of us lay there while the fifth got the drugs from the safe. A kick to the legs, a click of the pistols.

I remember thinking, 'I wonder if I'll get to finish this thought?' I knew it was a simple enough thing to die. Grandmother did. Some guys I went through school with were killed in a car accident the year after I left.

Some of the patients I'd cared for had died. I understood I wasn't exempt, but here I was, on the floor with two loaded pistols pointed at my head, held by a perpetrator capable enough to make it happen.

In the decades that followed, I've had visceral reactions to seeing guns, my startle reflex at being snuck up on was off the charts, and if I was in a public space like a café, I'd always try to sit without my back to the thoroughfare. Of course, I've come to understand that it was PTSD, but that was not a consideration back then. In fact, I was reproached by the Deputy Matron for asking for the next night off before days off. Thankfully, not so many years ago, a friend who had a licence to train others in firearms took me aside in a controlled environment and spent hours with me, teaching me how to handle and fire guns safely. Including pistols. It was a healing experience of one of the most disordering experiences of my life.

I'm so glad you survive this. Life is such an adventure and despite this experience and its immediate impact, you'll continue on your path in nursing and, with Caren, make a life in Brisbane. You'll still be something of a rarity, as a young man in a discipline made up primarily of middle-aged women. Yet it'll be in these settings where some of your greatest connections take place.

When you combine compassion with connection, it looks like palliative care nursing is a pretty good fit. Engaging with people at a time of vulnerability and fracture, there are so many opportunities for connection between people who are dying and those around them. The therapeutic relationship is what compassionate connection looks like. An interesting thing about connection in this setting is that it's brief but intense. You'll find that you're embraced by many families, your place in their home cherished and appreciated.

> *Jim was an old man whose time to die had come. His family – wife, two daughters and a son – were all involved in his care at home. Although I'm sure they had their struggles, they were calm and determined to enable Jim to die peacefully at home. I was their primary nurse and spent many hours with them in the last weeks of Jim's life. When Jim died, I attended the home to support the family. With his daughters, I helped wash and shave him, dress him in clean pyjamas, and prepare the room for the family and friends who were coming to say their last goodbyes.*
>
> *As we finished these last acts of care (which were of course for Jim's family as much as for him), one of his daughters turned to me and said, 'I never imagined something as beautiful as this was even possible. Thank you!' It was*

a humbling and deeply fulfilling moment. Precious time had been spent.

Later, I received a card from the same daughter, thanking me for my presence in their home during Jim's final weeks. It concluded with this message, 'If you ever doubt that you are out of place in palliative care, please remember what you did for Dad and us.' I still have that card.

You'll think for some time that it's weak to rely on the affirmations of others to build a sense of self, but they do help you. They acknowledge that your connections with those you'll have in your care bring out the best in you and others. There's always a risk that others will take advantage of this fondness to connect. Your self-confidence will ebb and flow over the years, but you'll become more self-reliant, and your sense of belonging will continue to be felt most strongly in these connections.

You'll work with a range of teams in the years to come. You'll be given your 'big break' in community palliative care with a small team of specialist palliative care nurses in Melbourne. The boss, Margaret, will tell you later that she 'took a chance on this young bloke' and you'll agree with one another that it panned out pretty well. She remains a mentor for much of your nursing career. Much of your community nursing will be done in Brisbane with the

Blue Nursing Service and you'll encounter many, many families whose experience of caring for a dying family member or friend will be enriched by your contribution.

Be prepared for connection to be the source of fulfilment and distress. Deebs and Marg are two colleagues who'll become dear friends – there's fun as well as heartfelt care amongst you. You make friends easily at work and although your enthusiastic personality rubs a few people up the wrong way, you'll bring energy and connection to every place you work. You're a kind-hearted bloke but your eagerness to connect makes you vulnerable to others whose motives you'll be oblivious to. There are some hard lessons to be learned in the years ahead – the hierarchy of healthcare will be a struggle for you, when you assume people are in healthcare with a common purpose. There'll be some friction, some hurtfulness given and received. A big relocation of your whole family for a big chance at advancement comes unstuck, due in some part to your own naivety, but also with some unscrupulous conduct from people you believed you could trust. Your life motto will help you navigate these experiences, but be warned, this is not the same as resolution.

A change of direction is coming too – in your late thirties, you'll move away from clinical care. It'll be by choice, but you'll feel pretty exhausted by the demands of community nursing, overnight and weekend on-call and team leadership at the same time that you're facing the challenges of fatherhood, a mortgage and the busy-ness of middle age. The change is into the world of research and your curiosity will fly in new ways with new people.

Curiosity

You're fortunate to have grown up in a house where curiosity was embraced. As a Dutch emigrant, your father's background – name, language, family – is fascinating to you. Perhaps your love (and eventual extensive collection) of atlases reflects your curiosity about the world beyond the small town you grew up in? Your mother's profession as a teacher has filled the house with books – biology, art, history, society, culture and religion are just some of those that capture your imagination, but you do absorb whatever information is around you. You're always learning, and this will be a lifelong disposition. So, you have your parents to thank for creating a home where curiosity was embraced.

> *In the acknowledgements section of my doctoral thesis, I recognise the contribution of my parents, Wim and Dorothy Rosenberg, who instilled in me from an early age the value of intellectual curiosity and created a home environment where both the encouragement and resources to pursue it were made plentiful. I honour these foundations and their enduring interest in my scholarly pursuits.*

You're in a hospital-based nurse training programme now and you'll go on to complete four university degrees (yes, four!). Your disastrous start to Year 11 will fade into obscurity as you pursue learning, both formal and informal. There'll be some remarkable academic successes ahead and you'll earn them. You'll figure out eventually that your learning style means that you have to comprehend the big picture to give context to the details. This is going to be challenging at times as you struggle to remember detail without context – learning *why*, not just *how*, is a critical shift that will happen between your hospital training and academic studies.

> *Why was it that I struggled to recall emergency procedures in critical clinical situations? Young Billy, who filled up his bed vomiting all the blood he'd swallowed following a car accident. Tanya returning from her surgery and having a respiratory arrest in the lift? So many examples where I just couldn't remember what to do. Thankfully, there were others around to respond and learn from, but despite all my curiosity, all the information I had in my head, why was this was amongst the hardest to retrieve?*
>
> *My friend and colleague Deb, who is both a nurse and a sociologist, once introduced me to other sociologists saying, 'John's not a sociologist, but he thinks like one.' It certainly explains a thing or two. I need to see the big picture. I*

need to understand the social contexts of disease and the experience of illness, dying and grieving.

You'll witness the emergence of two major new diseases in your career, and one is already near. A new transmissible disease called HIV leads to a terrible syndrome called AIDS. Like your colleagues, you won't know how it spreads, what it means for the future, or whether it will grow or fade. At the moment, it's almost always fatal, and you'll encounter many patients whose lives are coming to an end in really confronting ways, both in human terms but in clinical care settings too. Because so much is yet to be learned about AIDS, you'll enter patients' rooms during their terminal care suited up in mask, gloves and gown. It will become part of your palliative care work and as knowledge about the disease grows, so too does nursing practice change. Most importantly, you'll witness how critical connection and compassion are amongst small networks when mainstream healthcare (and palliative care) creates sadness and isolation. In time, you'll see how, as a discipline, palliative care fell short of its own intentions to provide compassionate end-of-life care to all who need it in its sluggish response to the suffering of so many.

Decades later, a new disease will also emerge. COVID-19, like HIV, is a viral disease that will puzzle, frighten and kill people, fracturing not just families and communities, but whole nations. It's a challenge you would never have imagined you'd have to face. Again, despite all the suffering and fear, its connections between people that changes how this new disease will be navigated. Despite all the challenges of a new and frightening disease, people make all the difference.

Your PhD is all about how communities work together to support people nearing the end of life, their families and caregivers, and those that matter to them. You're going to be something of a trailblazer, writing the first ever doctoral thesis in Health Promoting Palliative Care. It draws together your core values and demonstrates that providing palliative care *services* is just one piece of the puzzle for people who are dying. Living while dying is about so much more than the bit you do. Your work in communities reinforces that when you see people in their own homes.

> *Whose business is dying? This was a curious question for many of us thinking, researching and writing about palliative care in the early 2000s. In one of my journal articles, I wrote: 'The starting point for better understanding the home as a place of dying lies in the ordinariness of living, the ordinariness of belonging to communities. From the dying person's perspective, home is normal... Viewed from this perspective, the scene of death (at home) is characterised by normality, domesticity and familiarity... and challenges the healthcare professional to think differently about their place is this (dying) scene.'* [vi]

John, you're a clever bloke, so don't put yourself down about it, but you'll also come to understand the value of 'practice wisdom', and that theoretical and practical knowledge are not mutually exclusive. Do you remember the charge nurse of the medical ward saying, 'John, you spend too much time listening to patients' stories'? I suppose she was trying to say that you have tasks to do and all this listening was slowing you down. I guess it was true, too; there's a routine to follow and things to do, and it's important that you continue to learn that. But curiosity about people and their journeys through illness also leads you away from the high paced, high acuity nursing of intensive care and emergency (both of which will make you very anxious). A discipline of healthcare that actually *requires* a slower pace and a strong interpersonal connection is one of your paths into palliative care.

Your curiosity has you publishing in journals and presenting at conferences here in Australia and in other places over the world. This is a wonderful part of the journey, but you'll do well to always remember that when all is said and done, it's about people. It's the combining of head knowledge and heart wisdom that makes up the full picture.

> *I'd been a keynote speaker at a national conference about Compassionate Communities and there'd been some social media traffic about it. When I got home, an indigenous man from our local parkrun mentioned he'd seen something about it but wanted me to explain it a bit. So, I talked about how Compassionate Communities is a movement that promotes the connections between people within communities to provide compassionate support when dying and grieving is taking place. 'Oh yeah,' he says, 'we've been doing that for 60,000 years!' That one comment brings it home to me over and over again that what I'm so curious about in these contemporary times is also something ancient, something known deep in our bones.*

But you know something? For all the things you're interested in, for all of the fascination you have for the world around you and the people in it, for all your striving for answers, the most enriching part of being curious is the *not knowing*. The *pursuit* of understanding, spurred by your curiosity, is actually the thrilling part. You're going to come to cherish a small quote by a German philosopher, Rainer Maria Rilke, who said:

> *'Be patient toward all that is unsolved in your heart and try to love the questions themselves… the point is*

> *to live everything. Live the questions now. Perhaps you will then gradually, without noticing it, live along some distant day into the answer.'* [vii]

A few final words

Thanks for listening, John. You're a good listener, when you stop talking for long enough! You're going to tattoo a simple, six-word motto on your arm: *Be calm and full of hope.*[viii] You'll mark your skin with these words, not because you fulfil them but because they are what you aspire to. When things are anything but calm, take a moment to perceive what is happening around you, a judicious pause. And be hopeful. Not to 'wish for', in the sense of a quick fix or an easy answer, but to believe that there will always be a return to love. Not something soft and romantic, but what the Greeks call ἀγάπη (agápi) – esteem, benevolence; it takes patience and steadfastness. It might not always become known to you, but it's a worthwhile way to live, despite the risks.

These anchor points are deeply embedded in you. Connection is the 'place' where compassion is given and received. It's the place where curiosity is shared, explored, tested and refined. Hold fast to them, let them inform your reflections, your choices in life, your learning. They won't bring you an easier path necessarily, but there's great fulfilment in living by them.

John.

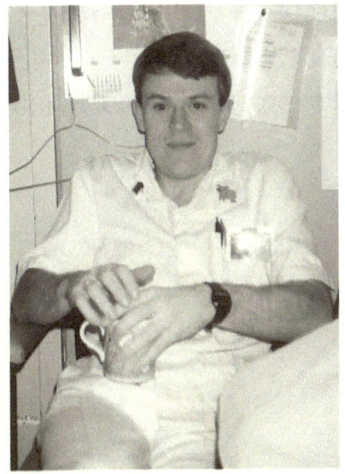 

About John:

John Rosenberg grew up in country Victoria and trained as a registered nurse at Wangaratta and District Base Hospital in the early 1980s. He eventually settled in Brisbane where he was a community palliative care nurse, until moving into the life of a nursing academic in the early 2000s. John was awarded a PhD in 2007 for an innovative study applying health promotion approaches to palliative care.

John currently works as a Senior Lecturer at the University of the Sunshine Coast. He is the current President of Public Health Palliative Care International, a global association promoting approaches to caregiving, dying and grief that engage whole communities in providing care and support.

John is married to Caren and is father to Lucy. A DIY tragic, he is usually found wandering his suburban oasis in search of new house and garden projects, even when the old ones aren't quite finished.

You can contact John at: johnrosenberg64@gmail.com

CHAPTER 2

Dare to Aspire

Judy Lonergan

I was born in Innisfail in 1955 and grew up in the sugarcane village, Wangan, with my sister, Susan. Domestic violence was a frequent part of our home life, and I regularly cared for our mother. Girlguiding was my lifeline. The Girl Guide leaders and the nursing staff at the Innisfail Hospital taught me basic first aid, how to care for a person, how to take a temperature and a blood pressure, how to wash a patient and how to make and change a bed. Nursing was my way out of this unhealthy situation and also to assist my mother and sister.

The opportunity came in 1968, when I saw an advertisement in the Innisfail newspaper for Cadet Nurses at The Royal Brisbane Hospital (RBH). I spoke with many family, friends and to my respected Year 11 science teacher, who responded with, 'Nursing, Judy! That's just cleaning up after people, you can do better.'

How wrong was he!

Instead of Year 12, I headed south from the cane fields and the bush to the big smoke of Brisbane.

More than 35 years later, I reflect on the numerous varied experiences, some life changing from starting as a cadet/enrolled nurse to becoming a preceptor/mentor to many nurses, some who are now Nurse Unit Managers (NUMs) and Directors in Nursing and it gives me a good feeling. I enjoyed the patient care contact while supporting nurses to grow in the oncology/haematology/palliative care disciplines, as opposed to managing a unit. As a result, I burnt myself out and then I became disappointed and angry when I retired in 2015. Knowing when it's time to move on in your career path is difficult when you find enjoyment in an area, and then don't move out of your comfort zone – you are left pondering.

Training and working through the hospital system was often challenging, but rewarding, when we had to improvise and learn on the run, and this still applies today. There were lots of camaraderie and fun which fitted in with the serious side of work. In the 1970's the sound of the ambulance trolleys moving across the wooden floorboards into the old RBWH Emergency Department (ED) set me into a mild panic because the charge nurse would go on her break with her silver drink canteen and cigarettes, leaving me to quickly assess and determine the patient's care. On one shift the emergency ward was saved from fire with a hosing down from the ward above, sausage sizzles from 4 am onwards! That was our nightshift team breakfast. Working in the ED was fun, interesting and challenging as one did not know what was going to happen on any shift.

I was nicknamed 'Clockwork Benham' by one of the night sisters, which upset me initially, but I didn't let her get to me. I worked out how I could get my patient's drugs checked so that my patients received their antibiotics/drugs on time. I was a stickler for time and my patients were my priority. My best friend, Erin, who was working on the ward below me, would ring three times after the supervisor had been to her ward. This gave me time to have all my drugs out ready to be checked. I didn't understand back in the seventies the term called 'the bigger picture' being in my case that the one-night sister/supervisor had four floors of wards to supervise.

The family is important to one's wellbeing, and back in the seventies and early eighties, working and managing a family was not easy. There were no childcare centres, so looking after children was my priority and I left nursing to look after my sons Allan and David until they were at primary school. With them settled in school I refocussed on nursing and completing a nursing refresher course in 1988 at The Townsville General Hospital. Working in the Medical Specialties Ward 4AB provided many experiences, such as caring for patients when the HIV pandemic occurred; caring for patients requiring palliative care, caring for Eddie Mabo prior to his return to Thursday Island, and caring for patients with respiratory and liver problems. I worked as a Level 2 nurse in Ward 4AB where my desire for haematology nursing was influenced by assisting the haematologist with bone marrow biopsies. Another colleague and I would put our hands up when this opportunity arose. My colleague won out more often than me, but when she was not around, that's when I grabbed the chance. I often cared for patients who were receiving their chemotherapy infusions, such as vincristine and cytarabine drugs. I also assisted with radiation oncologists and the medical oncologists' clinics. I really didn't know what I was doing in those clinics. I had no previous experience with day treatment clinics and was thrown in the deep end – a good way to learn.

Why choose oncology/haematology nursing?

In 1995 I grabbed the opportunity to be part of the Northern Oncology Service at The Townsville General Hospital at North Ward by joining the New Oncology Ward staff. The beginning of my cancer nursing journey. Little did I realise that working in the Medical Specialties Unit at The Townsville General Hospital was preparing me for my future in oncology/haematology nursing!

Whilst working in ward 4AB I watched the many patients who were diagnosed with any form of cancer go through so much adversity without complaining. Hence, the idea that I wanted to become involved in this area of nursing. Endorsing individualised patient care was my focus to provide safe and competent care whilst including family involvement. I also thought I could make a difference and that I would learn more about oncology and haematology so that I could become a blood stem cell transplant nurse.

I did not have aspirations of being a charge nurse/nurse unit manager; I just wanted to look after the patients and be a skilled nurse as well as look after my family. There are many nurses who want to be in charge but that was not my dream.

The new Oncology Ward was adjacent to the New Cancer Centre, which incorporated the Radiation Department, Outpatient Clinics and the Oncology Day Unit. I relinquished a level two position and applied for a level one position as I was very interested in learning about bone marrow transplantation and blood transfusions with the thought that I would be a bone marrow transplant nurse. Because I had a very young family I worked mostly night shifts, so that I could work and be part of my husband and sons' lives. These shifts were often very busy with about 16 blood tests to be taken each morning from 4 am. It usually took the three of us two hours to take all these bloods. There was the occasional emergency, but it was fun working with this nursing team. We handled most emergencies well.

Prior to the ward's opening in November 1995, a week's orientation from the 25th November 1995 until the 1st December was organised for the 17 nursing staff by the NUM Linda Barrett. Because of my love of Scotland, I often bantered with Scottish-born Linda, who was a great mentor. Her strength and resilience overcame many obstacles to ensure her staff were well educated and orientated in the use of new equipment, such as new IMED Pumps, the electric beds, the administration of chemotherapy and it's side effects prior to the first patient's arrival. She inspired me with the love of central venous access devices and was always pushing me to learn.

One day I administered a chemotherapy drug (Cytarabine) in the wrong order. The patient survived. My penalty was, researching and presenting 7+3 Protocol; Cytarabine/Idarubicin to the group with the pharmacist, medical staff and colleagues present. I never made that mistake again and I also learned to understand a protocol before I administered the appropriate drugs. Linda ensured we did basic monitoring of the patients who had leukaemia, including central line Management (which is integral to caring for these patients) who were having chemotherapy regimens which were very toxic and often debilitating.

Being nicknamed 'Judge Judy' by my younger colleagues added to the fun during the difficult, busy workplace. It was a steep learning curve for me, moving from caring for palliative care patients, watching Vincristine infusions and assisting the haematologist with bone marrow aspirations to thinking quickly whilst learning and maintaining safe practice and safe patient care.

In 1995, at the same time as the new Oncology Ward opened, I attended James Cook University to undertake a Bachelor of Nursing Science degree so that I could update my nursing knowledge, skills, and computer skills, which not only allowed me to work and assist colleagues safely but prepared me for research down the track. I'm not very good dealing with change, having trained through the hospital system and then through the university system. I knew that if I didn't learn to change, I would not be able to assist nurses within the hospital system. I learned that if I didn't change by integrating my hospital and university knowledge, I would not be able to assist nurses to grow and perform in the oncology/haematology unit within the hospital system. With this study behind me, I continued to pursue becoming (in my opinion), a good blood stem cell transplant nurse.

In 1998, Ms Sue Perrot took over from Linda as Nurse Unit Manager (Leader) of the Oncology/Haematology Ward and was forthright in ensuring the nursing team continually gained knowledge in the blood stem cell transplant discipline. With Wendy Trevarthen as the educator and The New South Wales College of Nursing, I completed the two-year Graduate Certificate in Oncological Nursing.

Participating in various groups such as the Oncology Nursing Group, Cancer Nurses Society of Australia, Transplant Nurses group, through which I went to the Royal Adelaide Bone Marrow Transplant ward 5D in 2003. Terry the NUM and staff shared plenty of BMT knowledge in between the sparring between the Lions and the Adelaide Crows filled me with knowledge and friendships.

Speaking at conferences transformed me from an introverted person into a more outgoing and fun person.

Often, I'd proudly say, 'I'm an oncology/haematology nurse,' whose interactions impacted significantly on the patients and their families. Sue constantly motivated me to want to learn more in the haematological area thus continuing my journey towards blood stem cell transplant nursing.

Sue Perrot was my major mentor. She guided me into the blood stem cell transplant area by assisting me to present at conferences; undertake an exchange to the old Royal Adelaide Hospital and relieve her as charge nurse in the Oncology Ward. Managing a ward is not easy with so many different and varied dynamics, dimensions, personalities and interactions involved. These things, Sue undertook very well always smiling and joking to keep us going in adverse times. Hence, why I looked up to her. Being a charge nurse was not for me, so returning to patient care and educating staff on the run was my focus. There were many times when I wanted to give up, felt anxious and even angry that I wasn't achieving well but the multidisciplinary staff within The Townsville Cancer Centre were supportive. They reassured me that life as a blood stem cell transplant nurse was Judy's career path.

2001–2005

In October 2001, The Townsville General Hospital moved from the Eyre Street, North Ward site to the Angus Smith Drive site opposite James Cook University. The convoy of Army Ambulances was a sight to behold. I escorted two mobile patients with intravenous infusions running in one of the ambulances, which was fun. The first 48 hours at the new site offered different challenges, such as monitoring intravenous infusions without pumps. Thanks to my hospital training where I monitored infusions successfully by counting the drips and thinking outside of the box was good. Other considerations, such as monitoring pain, discomfort, physical ability and diet could be addressed by connecting with the specific health disciplines.

It was a sad time when we closed the doors for the final time in the ward and left the magnificent healing views of Magnetic Island for views of Mount Stuart, bush and ongoing construction. A couple of shifts that I worked I found another use for urinals – catching little snakes which came up the drain holes in the sluice room, all part of the job on a shift!

Again, with Sue Perrot's encouragement, and in collaboration with a Clinical Lecturer at the Mater Education Centre, in 2002 I successfully completed a Stem Cell Transplant Course, which was a real bonus for me enhancing my opportunity in becoming a blood stem cell transplant nurse. Yay!

So, with the determination to improve myself, and to gain more experience and knowledge in the care of stem cell transplant patients I sought to go and work in the Haematology Unit at The Royal Adelaide Hospital (RAH). This also allowed me to spend time with my aunt, uncle and cousins living in Adelaide at the same time. My own belief was that South Australia was the leader in the fields of haematology, blood stem cell transplants and nursing care. Thanks to Terry (NUM, D6) and the nursing, allied health and medical staff from D6, I had a great time and educational experience. This was at the time, 2003 when the Brisbane Lions were winning their games against the Adelaide Crows, which enabled me to banter and connect with the staff enjoying AFL. I spent my days off doing home visits with the RAH Bone Marrow Transplant Team, where chemotherapy drugs and platelets were given at home. The way patients were prepared for transplants, was different to what we did at The Townsville General Hospital. After six months there I returned to The Townsville Hospital's Oncology Ward and shared the knowledge that I'd gained from my time in D6.

Haematologist Dr Nicholas Wickham from South Australia was highly knowledgeable in the blood stem cell transplant specialty. He was very helpful in sharing and teaching me about the different blood cell lines including how and why different conditions, such as leukaemia, aplastic lymphoma, multiple myeloma and Burkitt's lymphoma develop. As I was willing and wanted to learn he kept teaching me.

I had many opportunities to educate staff on the ward in basic patient assessment; management of blood stem cell transplant patients pre and post transplantation cares; the management of central venous access devices and managing blood product transfusions.

2005

I enjoyed orientating new nursing staff to the unit and collaborating with colleagues and the Nurse Unit Manager

(Sue Perrot), arranging preceptors for the new graduate nurses and the student nurses. At the same time, I would plan the various rosters to support the ward and the nursing staff. Also, I enjoyed supporting the staff during their three months of learning experiences. The plus for me was that I learnt from them especially as to how I could improve the future initial orientation education days whilst in the ward. If I could commence the orientation process to the Oncology Ward effectively and build strong relationships with the new staff, then together we should improve better outcomes for our patients. The good rapport that I had with the other educators within the Townsville Cancer Centre enhanced the education opportunities as well as the provision of appropriate support for colleagues, patients and families.

Communicating effectively with everyone, including visitors, patients, colleagues and all levels of the Townsville Cancer Team was and still is paramount. Furthermore, multi-disciplinary teamwork is integral to the service and through participation in allied health, other team meetings and journal club we evolved into an interconnected team, where all members are valued, involved and supported. When adverse events occurred, I coordinated regular debriefing sessions to ensure the team was well supported plus encouraged forums to ensure the service was always focused on the patients and their families. At the forums, team members were encouraged to discuss individual patients and share their feelings about the service we provide and how we might improve future care.

Keeping abreast with changes to practices was important to me and a requirement of the role of clinical nurse support in order to provide evidence-based care for patients. The Townsville Hospital Cancer Centre's Management Team were excellent forward thinkers and provided further education, which continued my journey to become a blood stem cell transplant nurse. Therefore, I undertook the Transition to Practice nurse education Programme in Cancer Care Nursing.

Technical and practical knowledge was gained by attending nursing conferences. Some conferences gave the opportunity to network with other likeminded healthcare professionals while at the same time focusing on yourself as an oncology/haematology nurse. Here a discussion on what everyone can bring to the world of those people diagnosed with cancer occurred. I would listen to case studies, such as those on prevention of chemotherapy errors in order to maintain safe practices in the workplace. For example, improved lighting in the medication/drawing up room, ensuring that workspaces were clear, that calculators with large buttons and magnifying glasses were available to assist with the reading of the chemotherapy drug orders which were often scribbled or written in the smallest print. This was very helpful for a person like me who needed reading glasses.

I also enjoyed making a poster about the research that the ward would undertake and then presenting the poster with a talk at a conference.

The Cancer Council Queensland, The Transplant Nurses Association and other healthcare organisations often offer nurses the opportunity to apply for a scholarship to attend a specific conference. Palliative Care Association, Queensland gave me this opportunity in 1996. The scholarship funded me to fly to Brisbane, attend palliative care workshops and visit Mt Olivet and other palliative care units around Brisbane.

My passion

My passion for central venous access devices (CVADs) enabled me to have fun at workshops, where I learned more about PICCs, vascaths, and Hickman lines (CLDs). During the early stages of the The Townsville Hospital Oncology Service, I assisted medical officers on the ward with the insertion of Hickman lines and vascaths. We had many blood fountains during an insertion, plus we saved many lives with these devices.

One Friday afternoon, I quickly learned not to turn my back after removing a patients' groin vascath because my fist was plugging the wound exit for 10 minutes, thereby reducing hemorrhage and saving her life. A great way to become friends! Whilst caring for patients with these CLDs I would often ponder what it would be like having one insitu. Practical experience was the best way for me to learn. It's not wise to think this way because at the end of 2007 I was diagnosed with right breast cancer after a lump appeared in around July 2007.

One day I discussed with my nursing friend Paula that I wanted to produce a document that would assist nurses and patients with the monitoring of their CVADs. So, together, and after many hours and months of formulating, reviewing and reformulating the form, in March 2003 The Townsville Health Service, Townsville Hospital printed out our form titled: Central Venous Access Device Flowsheet with the Queensland Government logo attached. What a proud moment for the Oncology Ward. I felt that finally I had contributed to something tangible to the Queensland Health hospital system.

Every year I met with my mentor, Sue Perrot (NUM-Oncology Ward 1997 to March 2011), reinforcing my goal and why I still wanted to be part of the team, and reiterated my poem:

- **Refocus on my healthy contribution to quality patient care in the TTH Oncology Ward and accept responsibility for maintaining healthy interpersonal relationships.**

- **Talk promptly with staff I have an issue with and ask for advice to communicate appropriately with the staffer.**
- **Be respectful of all staff regardless of job titles.**
- **Disengage in the blame and backbiting game and expect the same of others in return and concentrating on constructive staff criticism, overriding negativity.**
- **Accept staff as they are today. Forgive past problems and enable connectedness in order to find solutions to problems.**
- **No one is perfect. Human errors are opportunities, not for shame or guilt but for forgiveness and growth!**

(Commitment to my Co-Workers, Judy Lonergan, 2005)

July 2007 was an important milestone in the blood stem cell transplantation era at The Townsville Oncology Ward, The Townsville Hospital (TTH). I was happy as a bone marrow transplant nurse to join in the celebrations and to participate in the administering of the two-hundredth stem cell transplant.

Breast cancer journey

My breast cancer was misdiagnosed, and because of my working knowledge I kept pursuing tests during 2007 until I received a diagnosis on 22nd October 2007. Once diagnosed, all the healthcare staff were excellent. Some days were difficult as I'd worked with the consultants and healthcare staff before my diagnosis. They didn't want to inflict pain or see me get sick. I didn't mind students doing their assessments on me as I felt I was contributing to their future and learning.

I am very grateful to my colleagues and all the TTH staff who supported me and my family especially my sister, Sue, during my breast cancer treatment journey. I underwent six cycles of chemotherapy intravenously administered through a portacath. The treatment tired me and interfered with my cognitive functioning. In between each cycle I was allowed to work in the ward from the second cycle onwards. Occasionally whilst on a shift I would talk to patients who were scared to have their chemotherapy and reassure them by explaining what I was going through. They'd smile when I would take off my wig. After each cycle I would fly down to my sister, Sue, in Sydney who looked after me until I was well enough to return to work. I 'crashed' a couple of times, but nursing friends within the Oncology Ward always kept a check on me. It was hard for me to accept, not being my busy, useful self in the oncology area. People talk of hope; here my beliefs on hope were challenged. I would think, 'I am now a guinea pig' as no one knows for certain how long any one of us has to live. I often tried to have some fun during my treatment by arranging trivia nights and party days.

One day I went to work and was told I wasn't walking a straight line, so went home for the safety of everyone. I enjoyed my work so much that it was hard for me to see or let go or know when to get out and move forward in another direction.

Research projects and evidence-based care

Attending workshops, such as the Proteus Impact Leadership Course, taught me that I needed to embrace changes happening within the Healthcare System or once again I'd be left behind.

I enjoyed undertaking research projects and when I returned from RAH, I undertook a project titled: 'Central Line Insertion Site Dressing Trial with BD Persist (Chlorhexidine Impregnated Swab Sticks)'. The RAH used these sticks to prevent central line device site infections, and I also thought that the patients in the Oncology Ward at The TTH could benefit from the use of this product in their central line device care and providing evidenced-based care. The project received awards from the Research Department at TTH, but I felt my working colleagues didn't really care and the money we received went into ward revenue.

Also, I often worked on improving my understanding of people behaviours especially in relation to the reactions that can be expected from people when change occurs through participation in projects that have led to changes in practice, such as the 'Basic education programme for the Oncology Ward staff'.

Connecting with the Brisbane Nurses and other Queensland Regional nurses through being a member of the Oncology Nurses Group was another great platform to share knowledge and continue my oncology and haematology knowledge growth. I was able to present research projects at the conferences, learn speaking skills, enjoy delicious dinners and travel within Queensland as a proud Townsville oncology/haematology blood stem cell transplant nurse.

2011

From 2011 to 2012 another BMT learning opportunity came when David (NUM 5C at the RBWH) continued my blood stem cell transplant education. I was able to do this whilst every Wednesday I looked after my grandson, Riley, who is now 10 years old. In 5C I connected with many healthcare professionals at the RBWH who assisted me immensely. My central venous access device skills came in very handy here as well as the knowledge that I'd gained in Townsville. Here I cared for some patients who were from the Townsville Cancer Centre. They had a smile on their faces when they saw a familiar face, including my good friend, Tony, who was in 5C for his third BSCT.

Another challenging time was whilst a clinical nurse in the Oncology Ward, I was on long service leave, and a restructuring in the Queensland Health System occurred. Following several conversations with colleagues, I reapplied for the position of registered nurse and enrolled nurse support, which allowed me to continue blood stem cell transplant patient care and also educate nurses. This I undertook whilst also caring for the patients with a student nurse. This role in the Oncology Ward I happily committed to in May 2010.

I achieved my goal of becoming a blood stem cell transplant nurse. In a regional hospital the oncology and haematology patients are cared for in the same unit. This nursing in conjunction with my family was my life. There were many ups and downs, but nursing provided me with many opportunities, such as working at The Royal Adelaide and the Royal Brisbane and Women's Hospital's Bone Marrow Transplant Units.

Every May and September

Each year, May was the month when thanks to Paula we would hold Australia's Biggest Morning Tea at The Townsville Hospital where the healthcare staff, patients and visitors would come together and enjoy fundraising for the Queensland Cancer Fund, Cancer Council Queensland.

May was also the month where the hospital celebrated International Nurses Day, on the 12th, with nursing staff sharing their research projects undertaken or being undertaken.

In the sunflower month of September, I would encourage my colleagues to join me in participating in the 18-hour Relay for Life challenge once again raising much needed funds for the Cancer Council.

As the sun was setting over Mount Stuart, my palliative multiple myeloma patient, Lorac asked me (a nonsmoker) to roll her last cigarette. Having pushed her in the bed outside the Oncology Ward, I was quickly learning on the run how to roll tobacco in the paper. She enjoyed one puff smirking at me thankfully as the smoke blew into the red tinged sky. Then we quickly pushed her back smiling into her room so the family could share the farewell.

I enjoyed the connections that I made with the bone marrow transplant patients. One patient, Tony, and I connected in such a way that he donated a BBQ to the Oncology Ward and I would chase up the sausages and bread. The two of us would put on regular lunch time BBQs to raise money for equipment in the Oncology

Ward. This assisted patients through their treatment journeys, and it was great to see them all smiling.

Over the years there are many ethical dilemmas that one is confronted with. I was unaware of any complaints about my patient care until one day I received a call up to the manager's office to explain about a formal complaint.

I had to care for a patient, Stephanie, whom I had known very well within the healthcare system. She was being treated for bowel cancer with the tumour causing an obstruction in the upper bowel. As Stephanie presented with ongoing projectile vomiting, the oncology and surgical medical teams were preparing to take her to theatre at Stephanie's request. Also, the palliative care team had just become involved. Whilst all these plans were in progress, the family insisted on feeding her orally. She was vomiting after each oral feeding session. I then asked her son, 'Please don't feed Mum anymore,' but he kept on feeding her. A few days later I was called to management 'to explain'. I was within my rights to try and stop the family from feeding Stephanie, as my priority was to ensure Stephanie's comfort. I found out later that the family thought they were helping Mum and that this was their way of coping!

The upside of a complaint in nursing is when I occasionally received a thank you letter.

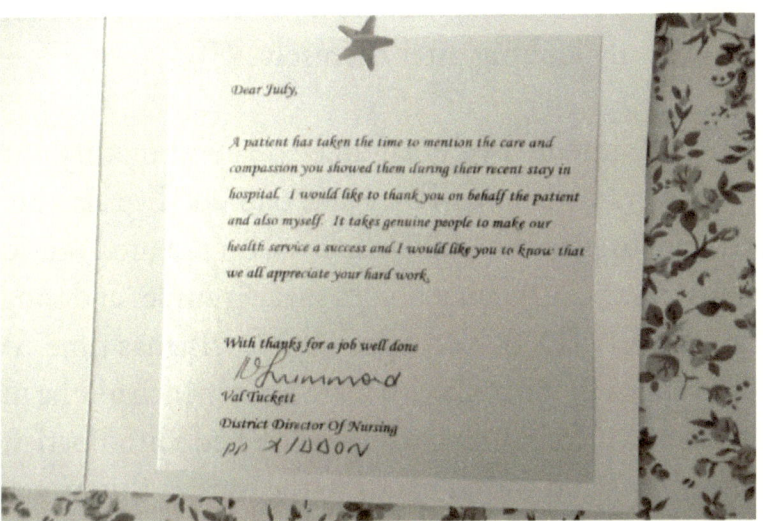

I have reflected on myself as an oncology/haematology nurse who did become a blood stem cell transplant nurse. When I turned 58 years old, I started to feel undervalued and useless at work. I did not understand the uniqueness of what I had contributed to, not only to the patients but to my coworkers until I retired. When you've been in a specialty for such a long time the people around you think you know a lot which is not always so. As I was getting older, I felt I was slower than the younger nurses coming through. Being an introvert didn't help. I was easily overstepped by the extroverted nurses. I should have used these feelings as chances to move into the education sector, instead of giving up. I felt that I'd given enough to The Townsville Hospital Oncology Ward. When your body and mind are tired, it is hard to know where to go as everyone else is at different levels in their healthcare pathway, all trying to look after themselves too.

This I think is 'burnout'. People try to care, but, in reality, they are only looking after themselves.

Since retirement, I've been able to spend quality time with my grandchildren Riley and Samuel. I've also been fortunate to play the ukulele (uke) with talented musical groups in various nursing homes sharing smiles and songs. Prior to COVID-19 I led a group at Christmas time. We played songs in the Palliative Care Unit, which all the uke players and I found rewarding when bedbound patients wiggled toes and waved hands to the music. This brought smiles to the families during their difficult time.

Listen to your mentors as they assist you along your path. Stop feeling like a victim and instead become the teacher and guide of your own destiny, which is not easy to do when storms are constant and variable. Understand that it's easy to celebrate the successes but difficult to learn the lessons.

Live life joyfully and simply continue to be a garden of opportunities for self-growth and happiness. Never give up, Judy. Especially never give up on the happiness, even if it involves continuing to overcome work/life challenges, for life is like a flower show: when some flowers open (opportunities), others close (career paths).

Survival tips for nurses:

- In the workplace you need to smile through adversities.

- Have a trusted someone outside of nursing with whom you can debrief.

- Connect with health care professionals who share similar values and beliefs to yours.

- Try to be prepared for the unexpected. This will come with experience and time.

- Follow your aspirations, be determined and find that inner strength to achieve them even if you have to travel through storms, difficulties, fatigue and disappointments.

- If you're a quiet person, don't succumb to the over expressive person.

About Judy:

Judy Lonergan is a retired clinical registered nurse who mentored many nurses in her 35 years of nursing. She enjoyed supporting oncology/haematology/palliative care nurses she worked with.

Judy was awarded a Queensland Cancer Council Award in Palliative Care Nursing (1995), a Townsville Diploma in Management, Graduate Certificate in Oncology Nursing and Stem Cell Transplantation, a Hospital Research Foundation research award in 2005 and nominated for The Hesta Nursing Award in 2011.

Judy now enjoys being a mother and grandmother who plays the ukulele.

You can contact Judy at: judy7lonergan@gmail.com

CHAPTER 3

A Passionate Purpose

Wendy Trevarthen

Dedicated to the humblest human I have known, Dad.

Hi there, Fuzzy Wuzzy!

Dad used to call you this when you were little. It stuck after being born in New Guinea, a surprise for Mum, Dad and Anne, and thereafter a blessing in disguise! Little did you know then how much passion you would have for others in your life, and that you will, time and time again, put others wellbeing well ahead of your own.

And now you have done it!

You have been successful in your application to enter nursing school at the Goulburn Valley Base Hospital. You are about to don your first blue pin-striped uniform with its crisp starched cap, like the one that you used to see watching *The Young Doctors*. That proud single stripe telling everyone you are a neophyte. But get that image out of your head. It's not real. It's a fictional depiction of what a seventies society thinks a nurse should look like. It does not show the end of shift 'rift', with sweaty underarms and dishevelled hair, the look of anguish of not getting everything done as expected (whose expectations?) and the wondrous look when you see the next fresh shift walking in to take over from you.

I recall the senior nurse educator at the interview, tall, thin, spinster-like in her mannerisms, and I imagined that she was a gentle, but firm 'charge sister' in her day. On point with her words, with a soft tone that indicated her empathy and compassion for others. She had been in the nursing education department for quite some time. She quickly tapped into my reasons for becoming a nurse, as I had not really worked them out up until that point.

Dad.

I told her my story and the impact that those feelings had on my decision to embark on the profession that has been in my blood ever since.

The beginnings

Who would have thought that when that man walked into where you were waitressing at Wahring Cottage Victoria, in mid-1985, it would lead to a conversation that would prompt you to apply for nursing. Something that you had briefly considered when Dad was sick, but pushed it aside as you thought you were not good enough? Not a Victorian native but raised in Tasmania and hijacked to Victoria by your heartstrings.

Why didn't you think of nursing two years earlier when you were a bit in a bit of a quandary of what to do with your life, when Dad was in hospital with all those medical professionals around? That would have been the ideal opportunity to take a good look, to see what was required, what hard work it is, both physically, mentally and, above all, emotionally.

But you were overwhelmed at that time. So much was going on. Dad lying there with tubes in his nose and his mouth, and you walked into that ICU room for the first time after he collapsed at home, wondering what the heck was going on. It was the day after Australia won America's Cup in 1983; you got up to watch this with Dad early that morning.

It was so much for you that you fell to the ICU floor and lost 10 minutes of your life, only to be woken in a hospital bed in an adjacent room by the lovely ICU nurses. Looking back, I don't understand how they spent so much time with you, when it was such a busy place, along with Mum in all her worry and shock, and our sister, Anne, explaining things as best as she could. After all, she was the nurse in the family. How Anne kept her cool was a strategy I was yet to learn.

> *It was so difficult to see him lying there, defenceless. What was this thing called Guillian-Barré Syndrome? We had never heard of it. I can remember the look in Dad's eyes. Just staring at us in amazement and owning that 'what the heck was happening to me?' look. But he was also telling us in those same eyes 'not to worry, that everything would be okay', but it wasn't.*

That day changed your life forever and it will make you realise over the years, how precious life is. Here one day, gone the next. Dad never returned to the physically abled, strong man that he once was, to be left quadriplegic, to lose memory of those 14 months in ICU, tracheostomy, ventilated, and then traumatised by the long recovery home...

Guillian-Barré Syndrome is awful. It attacks the myelin sheath of your nervous system and little did we know that Dad was going to endure this from his time in Vietnam in 1971, developing a compromised immune system to become unwell 12 years later and develop this mysterious syndrome. It was through no fault of his own. Serving his country and then being struck down at midlife during his peak, and at a time of us all needing a steady influence. How this affected my life was immense. I know that this family tragedy became my future benchmark, to realise that every day you have on this earth is a blessing. Living each day to it's fullest is what I aspire to. Don't waste your time.

Mum and Anne knew that you would follow your heart after leaving Tasmania and make a path of your own. You will always have a stubborn independent Scottish streak, determined to achieve some great humanitarian cause. Through that personal experience over many years, you really will show how you care for your fellow human. That is the core value that will take through your life with every connection you make and every colleague you meet.

So, congratulations on getting through your interview and being successful with your enrolment.

Your journey is just about to begin.

The Three Amigos

Those two nurses (out of a group of 18) that you are about to meet are going to take you through your three years and beyond. You will not be in the same shoes, but you will travel with them throughout your clinical rotations. Medical, surgical, paediatrics and then in the more advanced specialty areas. Even though they won't be physically next to you on each shift, as the junior nurses in the surrounding hierarchy, you certainly will share experiences with them during shift rotations on your days off and when you go back into your study blocks. They are going to be there to brainstorm and learn from. You also will share the gossip and camaraderie, and find solace in your inner thoughts that you don't really want others to know about!

Swapping shifts will be possible with them because they are the same level as you. You will have that ability to be able to swap your shifts around if you are wanting to get that weekend off, have a particular night off, or to minimise those 'late/early, late/early' sequences that the junior nurses always seemed to get. You will support each other to ensure that there is a life beyond those clinical walls.

During your second year, you will be doing a six-week mental health placement at an institution called Mayday Hills in Beechworth, Victoria. Having a mental health hospital with the name like that conjures up horrid thoughts even before you start. This was prior to the big transition to have mental health clients incorporated into the general community.

> *The clients were extremely institutionalised, and I can remember feeling so frightened even to walk through the grounds of the hospital. We knew there was security around, and our nurses' quarters had locks on the doors, so we could lock ourselves in. I do recall tapping on my amigos' walls in the middle of the night as a way of saying, 'Are you OK? Are you still there and don't forget me?' We heard halfway through this placement the nurses' quarters housed ghosts, just another thought to contend with.*
>
> *The institution had been there for quite some time. Some of their work practices and workflows were questionable compared to todays' standards. I remember each building housed a different 'type' of mental illness, and looking back, it was like walking through something out of a Stephen King novel. We didn't know any different, but we talked about feeling sorry for the way the patients (or clients) were being treated. I made sure I was never alone. I spent a lot of time looking at patient's histories to gather prompts for the assignment due at the time, just to escape the reality of what I was seeing.*

> *Mental health is something that I had little exposure to as I was growing up, it was kept out of society, 'hush, hush!' So trying to understand this in such a short period of time was completely foreign, frightening and outside my comfort zone. I decided then and there that I was not going to go down that career path. Logic and science were my comfort zones and that is where I will stay. Looking back though, I felt I could have asked more questions, talked more with the nurses (although some of them I thought were interestingly eccentric!) and be more open minded about the whole experience. It was all a bit of a blur, and specific situations are now hard to identify. The brain does protect you against harmful situations, it seems.*

Sharing that experience with those two other nurses will make it easier. One of the things that is so different between nursing back then and at this time that I'm writing to you, is how much that support has changed over the years. During your three years of training, you will come across different nurses to connect with and reintroduce yourself to new nurses each time that you go on clinical rotation, building your network.

The ability for you to quickly introduce yourself to your colleagues, building trust and rapport, is really important. That initial connection and the way others see each other for the first time plays a big part on how they will perceive your time together. One of the advantages of going through nursing together, as a trio and within in such a small group, is that you will make those strong connections and build those connections over your three years. This will carry you forward into your future years.

Make a good impression, show up on time, have a high standard of presentation, dress, speech, be curious, apply what you have learned and seek more information as needed.

Let it snow!

You will develop a social circle outside of nursing that is vital to build those relationships and have that bit of fun during downtime as a part of your overall wellbeing. This will help you cope with the demands of your nursing training. I can foresee ahead one trip that you are going to have with these two amigos and their friends.

> *It's hard to imagine that growing up in Tasmania I didn't have the wonderful experience of skiing down any mountains during winter. No, I was too busy getting frostbite on my fingers playing netball with my other pals, peeling out of my 'tracky daks' to just a skort and shirt, moving around just to stay warm. When one of these three amigos suggested we go skiing at Mr Hotham, just*

a couple of hours drive away one frosty winter morning, I jumped at the chance.

Looking quite the part in winter woollies and all cramped into the one car, off we went. I discovered that there were certain things that needed to be experienced to be able to ski properly. One of them was to 'place' yourself (rather than sit) onto the chairlift.

Splat!

Onto the ground to be embraced by snow.

The other was that to go down the hill, one had to be pushed by the 'friend' of one of the amigos, whether I agreed to it or not.

No choice, the only way was down, and in a hurry!

Coached by one said friend of one amigo, I quickly learned that the pace you travelled was directionally proportional to the angle your skis were with one another. (See, everything is a science!) I decided that once at the bottom, that one experience showed me that my skills were better utilised in making snowmen rather than skiing, and that was the best thing about the day. The fire and the lunch with a hot chocolate came a close second!

Aye, the little people!

I can share with you during your second and third year in paediatrics that you witnessed such things that we don't see too much of now due to immunisations and preventative medicine.

I witnessed children in their humidicrib, suffering with things such as whooping cough, croup, and nursed children with diseases such as the measles. I recall horrible sights and sounds and pray that those sounds never emulate from my own children or grandchildren.

I can recall the charge nurse of paediatrics as being someone to be quite fearful of, and rightly so. What an important level of responsibility to have so many little ones and managing the different levels of nursing staff caring for them. She was right onto any miscommunication or misadventure each time before anything happened.

One little slip, one little blip, one scoop too many or too few in the baby's formula and she was right there on to it. I do recall that there was an enrolled nurse (EN) that was pretty much her to 2IC. Yes, that's right, an EN was her wingman, and I am grateful to have learned so many things from our EN colleagues.

So many of our basic nursing skills were taught to us by the ENs who had been on those wards for a long period of time. They were our measure of safe basic nursing care, reinforcing those primary nursing skills that we learned. You will discover that these skills are loosely embedded in our current registered nurse (RN) graduates, especially those who have not taken on side work as assistant nursing roles while studying. When we came out onto the wards the ENs were the ones that were the greater teachers. The new RNs seemed to be too busy trying to get their head around their roles, whereas the ENs were the ones actually on the floor and gelling things together.

> *I didn't have children of my own at that stage, and to look after somebody else's child, when I had little experience with those tiny bodies, was frightening. I was constantly learning about communicating and turning a procedure into something that could be fun, when in fact it was terribly serious. Every chance that I had to communicate with these little people was such a wonderful learning opportunity.*

You are going to come across children that have hip dysplasia, are part of a domestic violence situation and have anatomical disfigurations. Such awful diseases and situations, but these little people just continue, they want to be smiling all the time. You can't help but wonder where does that sense of laughter and the smiley face come from? Indeed, they are brave little soldiers.

You will also see later, after you graduate, children on the burns unit following some sort of accident. Your role there will be to promote healing and rehabilitation, to calm the children and the parents, to educate the families to give them the opportunity to heal physically and mentally in a safe place.

I recall one incredibly sad case where an overjealous sibling turned the hot water on her younger sister while in the bathtub, and she was unable to get out. The parents were none the wiser as they mentioned that they often heard the two girls squabbling with each other while in the bath together. That poor child, scarred for life, and the ongoing challenges she was to endure in not knowing if she would be able to bear children in the future. Five minutes of inattention for a lifetime of struggle, treatment, and subsequent grafting as she aged.

I recall caring for young toddlers, burned from being over curious with combustion wood heaters, or falling on to an unprotected fire, resulting in burns on the palms of their little hands. Once the initial phase was over, they did not mind having their hands in little plastic bags for

> *a while until the blisters went down or were debrided, and then subsequently skin grafted. Playing games with their bandaged hands was important for them to heal and restore function as they healed and grew.*

As a part of working on the burns unit you will spend some time in ICU, learning about fluid shifts, and advanced airway management. It is not until your older years do you realise that during that time, a lot of information will waft over your head, as a coping mechanism. Flashbacks of Dad being in ICU will be common during those short weeks, and you will discover that ICU/ED, or even surgical nursing, simply will not be on your radar for future career options.

You will, however, develop a curiosity around burns healing, which will make you gravitate later in your career towards working in the radiation oncology area.

What is cancer?

Cancer nursing – the bits they don't tell you

During your training, you will have rotations to the general medical and surgical areas. There will be no specialist renal, endocrine, or respiratory unit as there are today. These will be mixed together to make a 'liquorice all-sorts of wards', within the medical or surgical areas. But one thing was missing from your training… cancer nursing. It will be touched on in theory during your third year, but not covered in depth, and little do you know that it is going to form a great part of your career in the future!

So, your training will be just the beginning of your journey. Your career will take you, by default, and by way of personal curiosity, into the area of oncology. That high school fixation with the periodical table and applying those letter symbols to treating people with cancer will get the better of you.

Little would you know that at the end of your training you will have a misunderstanding that cancer relates to one disease, and this misinformation was quite common at that time. You will discover that it relates to many, many diseases. Solid tumours, haematology or blood and lymphatic cancers and some cancers of which the origins are unknown. You will nurse acute care patients through their treatment and subsequently towards the latter part of your career – palliative care.

So much so, that you will be successful in a scholarship that will take you halfway around the world to study radiation oncology at the Royal Marsden Hospital in London. What an exciting trip that will be, meeting nurses from the Greater London region, and learning how these patients were treated and managed by radiation therapy. You are going to come across many experienced nurses who will be role models for you, including your preceptor in your first area of oncology who inspires you to learn more about oncology nursing.

You will witness the evolution of cancer treatments within your lifetime. Early detection through advancements in screening, improvements in the way cancers are treated, and the long term sequalae that are now evident. Survivorship and ongoing discoveries will seem like science fiction becoming reality. It is during your career that cancer treatment will evolve into a speciality of its own, from its origins by default following the nuclear episodes during World War II and our earlier pioneers such as the Curies.

> *Who would have thought that I would develop a personal flair for this type of nursing? I don't really think earlier in my career I would have been ready to tackle such a difficult area. I guess it was my empathetic nature and my ability to connect with and read people at various times during their lives and seeing through my personal experiences how important it was to listen, to go with the flow with the interactions and not feeling guilty or pressured by the constraints of time. Giving those families and the clients the care and attention they needed during such a critical time is essential, and just as important as an accurate assessment or performing a specific clinical skill.*

You are an emotional being and you are going to take on these scenarios, giving 100% each time. It is the challenging patients, as well as the uncomplicated ones, that help you to respond to these emotional journeys in a professional way, and you will put a little bit of you with each interaction that you make.

Over time, you will build resilience and learn. My advice to you is to be present at every interaction with both your patients, their families, and other nurses' reactions. If you feel that that a patient is not getting 100 per cent of the care and attention that they deserve, that you do speak up and advocate for them.

Client advocacy

I remember one time I was working a late shift on a ward that had not caught up with the times. It must have been in the middle of summer as I recall it being very hot and humid. It was on an open ward of 12 patients separated by cotton curtains, stainless steel over bed tables and floor to ceiling bay windows with a balcony beyond. Four levels up, the windows were opened to allow some venting breezes through, with the curtains bellowing in and out, a metaphor of what was to come.

The four-bed male bay had one indigenous man who I recall was shy, only communicating when it was meaningful to him. I recall he had no visitors, a loner from a faraway distance. Looking back on it now, I think he was in shock just being in a hospital. He had chronic obstructive airway disease (COAD), but I just had this feeling there was something more that was wrong with him. His body was extremely thin, with the remnants of homemade tattoos on his arms and legs and scars on his chest, that looked like tribal markings. His skin was leather-tough, weathered by the Australian outback.

The first half of the shift was uneventful, routine observations showed nothing out of the ordinary, but after darkness fell, this man became more short of breath. He kept on indicating that he was 'ok', gesturing 'thumbs up', and indicating he wanted to be left alone, 'shooing' me away with his hand signals. However, he allowed me to continue to take his observations, and I felt he could understand my concern when I started taking them more frequently. Sure enough, his respiration rate continued to climb, along with his heart rate and initially his blood pressure too. I recall using the paediatric cuff around his skinny arm.

My team leader seemed concerned but did not want to bother the doctors, saying, 'We'll continue to monitor for a while.' Which I did.

Next round of observations indicated even higher numbers and that gut feeling began to gnaw at my insides. I expressed that I thought we should ring the medical team. Unsupported by my team leader, she commented, 'Go ahead and ring them yourself,' which I did. Sure enough, I was berated and belittled by the resident for bothering him. 'Keep monitoring,' came his response. It was close to the end of the shift for both myself and the resident and I could read between the lines. I gave him a detailed account of the changes over the course of the last hour, and by this time my patient was quite distressed with his breathing.

Ventolin had no effect. I was getting nowhere and getting more and more frustrated. Out of the depths of my frustration came the words, 'If you don't come and review him now, I'll be contacting the consultant on call for his opinion.' My team leader's jaw dropped, and I recall her snatching the phone from my hands. She then embarrassingly concurred with my assessments and encouraged the resident to review. Two minutes later, he was on the ward. Within five minutes, a mobile X-ray unit was clattering through the ward, waking up everyone along the way. Sure enough, the gentlemen had a tension pneumothorax and needed an intercostal tube inserted for release of the accumulated air. The oncoming shift were keenly interested in what was happening and handover was delayed by half an hour while we

> *set about getting this man to ICU overnight for further monitoring and the care he deserved at least an hour prior. We all then went about settling the ward down again for the night.*
>
> *I reflect on this often and do not want to think about the reasons why others did not want to do the best for this man. He deserved the care and attention that everyone else should receive, and I felt proud of myself for not only following the right procedures, but also trusting that gut instinct, that prompted me to be curious and speak up.*

So, as you look back on these experiences, keep your wits about you, continue to question if it is not sitting well with you and support yourself with your data, as sometimes others need to follow your lead to enable them to have the strength to go forward. Don't listen to anyone that minimises your concerns for your patients, but rather make sure to advocate professionally to ensure your patients are kept safe.

Glass half full

There are going to be so many experiences in your nursing career that will give you joy and inspiration, allowing oxytocin to flood your system which will give you great sense of satisfaction. You are fortunate enough to be training at a time where you do an apprenticeship style of training, learning so much on the job. You are going to have rotations through various specialties that are going to open your eyes to areas that a lot of nurses currently (unfortunately) don't experience during their undergraduate degree. Your training will follow a logical pathway, linking theory to practice within recent memory, so that you can apply what you are learning straight away. It just made sense.

Someone is going to tell you down the track that you always have a glass half full approach, and say it in such a condescending way, implying that you that you need to look at the other half empty glass as more of a priority. Stick to the glass half full approach. It works every time, but be mindful at the same time of the half that is empty. Some people just do not want to top up their own glasses, despite you leading them towards it.

You are going to discover that people have different personalities and different ways of expressing themselves. Some feel comfortable about openly talking about things and others are shy but find their own time and their own way to process things. You are an introvert at heart. You like to have your own space and time; you have dreams to achieve great things in your life, to fulfill some sense of a greater purpose, but due to your quiet manner and silent achiever status, you often get overlooked.

But you do recognise that at times you need to step outside of that comfort zone and make yourself known to say what's on your mind or keep things safe. You can set yourself a task or focus on a particular issue to be able to get your point across. However, sometimes it may come a little too late and then the frustration bug bites you. Mind your words, young Fuzzy Wuzzy, and be mindful of who is hearing them. You may see your ideas developed by others as a result. Be thankful in knowing that they are benefitting patients in the longer term. Your ego will be satisfied in knowing this.

There is a lot of emphasis placed now on integrity, trust and respect, and you will develop the ability to put your words in such a way that your integrity is maintained. Providing your communication and your facts stay solid, then you should have no problems. Getting your point of view across and recognising your boundaries is key. So, knowing when to step in and when to step out is essential. Create boundaries for yourself using the 'circle of control' method.

You will use this 'circle of control' for your own problem solving and share this with many other nurses over your career. Many will come back to you afterwards and show their appreciation to you for sharing this with them.

In the world of education, nurse education roles have evolved to be a facilitator of learning rather direct hands-on teaching. When I was a nurse educator at the Townsville Hospital, I was involved with the Apheresis training. This project involved the nurse unit managers (NUMs) of the units, the supplier of the Apheresis equipment and the education department (which was my role covering the oncology area). It is a remarkably interesting area of nursing, and an attractive skill set to have if you are wanting to be involved with haematology nursing. To be selected to do this training was a recognition of your advanced skills in cancer nursing, and your ability to perform procedures at an exceptional level.

The role definitions of the nurses involved in this project proved to be the boundaries of who would be involved. While I had a strong interest, it was outside of my role scope (my circle of control) to be directly involved with the education delivery. I was in control of the framework of the education programme; I had influence over the details of the programme and expressed my ideas over the way it could be implemented. The final decision for the latter fell to the NUMs. So, in this example, you can see how boundaries of control, influence and concern came into play. I personally would have loved to have become competent in this area, but I put this aside for the benefit of reaching a stage where there was a service provided to patients with the appropriately trained staff.

So, young Fuzzy Wuzzy, you will have to put that ego aside sometimes, look at the broader picture, and do what you can within your 'circle of control' that you have direct responsibility for.

Knot in a big bow tie

Your career is going to take you on a journey from not only being clinically based but having broader opportunities to develop your skills. The beautiful thing about being a nurse is that you can develop along many different pathways: stay clinically focussed, move into education, management, quality, research and now, even digital and technological opportunities are emerging.

Later in your career you will follow a leadership and management path. You will be responsible for many staff, many clients and will become involved in two capital works programmes (Townsville and Gold Coast). Exciting opportunities ahead at such an important level and contribute towards these healthcare facilities of the future.

These experiences will allow you to grow, both personally and professionally, but along the way you will be squeezed from below and above, meeting demands of both the staff, clients and their communities, and the hierarchy, while trying to maintain standards, deadlines, and expectations of others, as well as your own.

> *I often said to others that I felt like 'a knot in a big bow tie' being pulled at either end to make a perfect bow, without others acknowledging the learning and the hard work involved in achieving the outcome.*

Because you will be afforded so many opportunities, you will get a little bit confused as to what your career direction or path will be. It is like picking oranges off a tree when all of them are ripe for the picking. This will seem to be the way forward in your career, taking these opportunities as they arise, and indeed this will be encouraged.

However, you will not follow the one mentor all the way through your nursing career. So, in retrospect, my advice to you is to seek out one or two main mentors, who are open-minded across the wider opportunities that exist and who can give you the direction that you need without being biased towards their own career progression. You may need to look beyond your direct clinical area for this, but they must recognise your core abilities and have your best interests at heart. Stay in touch with them. Use your reflections to guide you. Stay true to your values and tap into your strengths to determine where you will thrive.

Stay in touch with the core skills that you will develop during your training. Stay in touch with the caring kind of approach that you have and that humanity within nursing that draws a greater majority toward this profession.

Avoid developing 'helicopter arms' in a busy environment. Use the standards of your nursing to critically think around the situation that you see in front of you and prioritise appropriately. Communicate well with your colleagues and recognise that what is not perfect one day, will be on another.

Finale

It's 2021. So much has changed since you started. From caps and stockings, to scrubs and practicality. From putting water in manual wall mounted nebulisers to outbreaks of diseases that have not yet evolved.

We are now living amidst a global viral pandemic like the ones we read about in cartoon magazines during our childhood, straight out of the author's imagination. You will live through others – HIV, Ebola, Anthrax and the evolution of nuclear medicine, to now a virus so dangerous it has put us into total isolation from the outside world and each other – Covid-19.

And it is through these times that nurses, the backbone of our global healthcare systems will continue to foster connections with each other, our clients, and our communities. Gelling them together with the essentials of life, saving lives, promoting healing and conversely enduring end of life. Nurses are great problem-solvers, inventors, menders and healers. We need to keep this alive, to nurture the very existence of our profession.

You will make a difference in the world, one person at a time.

Your biggest fan,

Wendy T

XXX

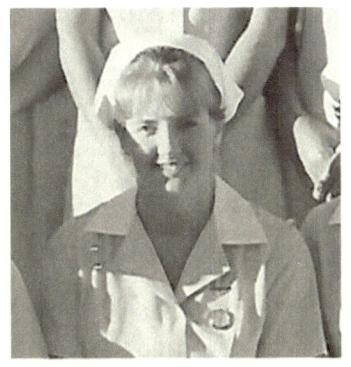 

About Wendy:

Wendy Trevarthen is a registered nurse, mother, grandmother, partner and mentor to many. She has been involved in healthcare all her career and has seen firsthand the dramatic effects of chronic illness on the patient and their extended family members. Indeed, her journey, like many other nurses, started with a personal family tragedy.

Awarded with two Queensland Cancer Council Awards, including study at the Royal Marsden Hospital, London, Wendy has extensively applied her knowledge and skills throughout her career in many roles: clinical, managerial and education, in both acute and community care across three Australian states.

As an educator, she has imparted her knowledge to student nurses, post-graduate nurses, and colleagues. Combining her experience spanning over three decades, she continues to strive for patient advocacy integral within the heart of the nursing profession.

She is committed to lifelong learning, converting her Hospital Certificate to a Degree in 1994, and achieving a Postgraduate Certificate in Cancer Nursing in 2009. She has continued to study at the post graduate level, embarking on a Nurse Practitioner Masters Course in 2010, but unable to complete this due to what she calls 'shifting goal posts beyond her control'! She is now continuing a similar path in Health Education.

If you would like to be a part of future volumes of *Dear Nurse Me (or its equivalent)*, reach out for the opportunity to share your story and the lessons you have learned.

You can contact Wendy at: wendy@healthyoptionsnow.org

CHAPTER 4

Finding Your Niche

Desley Joyce

Dear Kershaw,

It seems surreal that, 40 years on, I am writing this letter to you. High school is over and the next chapter of your life is about to begin. It has now been eight years since you moved to Mareeba where you spent most of your schooling. Although it is with excitement that you look forward to moving to Townsville, it is with some sadness as you will miss your family and friends. There were feelings of grief leaving a close friend who had terminal cancer as you knew it would probably be the last time that you would see him. It was organised that your mother would contact the local Townsville catholic priest to tell you when he passes away. The catholic church had always been a part of your school life where you had found comfort through many hard times. In amongst this sadness, little did you know that there was a big adventure on your doorstep. There are many friendships that will be made as 50 nurses commence their General Nursing

Training on 16th February 1981 at The Townsville General Hospital (TGH).

On the first evening sitting on the balcony of the nurses' quarters, you began acquainting yourself with some of your future nursing colleagues. The nurses sat in little groups and asked each other questions about each other. There were some who were shy and some who took the stage. You were taking the modest route and contributing here and there. The nurses' quarters were located in a six-storey building which overlooked a carpark and you could see the arrival of all those who were entering or visiting. The carpark was very busy on that day, as most of you were settling into your new home or at least it would be for the time being.

The next eight weeks will be spent completing the Preliminary Nursing Course (PNC), which mostly takes place in the classroom preparing for your entry onto the wards. Initially you were to be called Nurse Evans, but as there were other nurses with the last name Evans, you took your mother's maiden name and were known as Nurse Kershaw-Evans. Your grandmother was so proud that she rang asking to speak to Nurse Kershaw-Evans. As you were not home, a message was left for you. As you arrived home there were a few giggles over this. The name Kershaw has stuck, with one friend still calling you Kershaw today.

Finding Your Niche

It was exciting for you as you were fitted with uniforms. The first pay day came, and your board was around $30 a fortnight. This included the laundering of uniforms, meals in the dining room at the main hospital and rent at the nurses' quarters. Looking back, you think this was a great perk as all expenses were covered. This is very different to university-based nursing education as it is today with nurses having to travel to do their practical and find their own accommodation.

Three weeks into PNC you were sitting in the education building on break when you saw a priest walking towards you. Instantly you were filled with fear of what you were about to hear. After hearing what the priest had to say you adjourned to your room in the nurses' quarters where a few colleagues checked in on you. There was a sudden feeling of peace in amongst the grief as deep down you knew he was finally at peace. That evening you fly to Cairns where your older brother, Paul, picks you up to drive you to Mareeba where you stayed until after the funeral. Paul and his wife, Isa, were on holiday at the time in Mareeba. Paul and Isa are also nurses. At this time Paul was also completing his nursing training at TGH and was a year ahead of you.

Life was about to change as you entered the wards. All student nurses were part of the staff allocation, so this meant although you were under the supervision of a registered nurse (RN) you were responsible for the direct care of patients within your scope. Although extremely proud in your uniform the experience would not be without its challenges. Missing time in PNC by attending the funeral did not help. Ward allocations were usually in six-week blocks with various blocks of classroom education. Every ward move meant a new learning curve. It also meant working with different colleagues and learning the new expectations of those with whom you were working with. Your first allocated ward was the Private ward. Paul was also working on the same ward at the time. This becomes an advantage for you, but maybe not for him. You were feeling scared to ask questions for fear of being seen as inadequate. That meant you would ask Paul. There was an occasion that you had a piece of anatomy mixed up with another and you approached Paul before asking the Sister in Charge. Paul was horrified at the thought of the latter once the question was asked of him.

Shift work and managing workloads were a struggle for you. You remember well working 10 continuous night shifts. Nursing presents new challenges every day and no day is the same. As a junior nurse, a lot of time was spent in the pan room. There were very few sterilisers around at that time so the pans would be scrubbed and soaked. You would often say that the only place your name would ever be in lights is over the door of the pan room.

At the end of each stint on the ward came the ward report. This could be stressful as sometimes you were not given feedback until then. Although you would try

Finding Your Niche

extremely hard it was not always resulting in a glowing ward report. There were disappointments for you but was your expectation of yourself too high? Most of you had just left school and getting used to discipline of this unique type was a culture shock. Time management was a struggle as often you were learning the ropes and having to juggle the day-to-day challenges in caring for your individual patient cohort. There were quite a few times that you think of leaving. This was generally when you hadn't quite cut the mustard and the ward report was not what you expected. You would often go and find Paul to have a discussion. The standard conversation was, 'You could always work at Pizza Hut.' They always seemed to be advertising. In saying that, it was a standard joke and Paul was supportive.

Living in the nurses' quarters meant that you usually had someone to debrief with. There were some very close friendships developed. Debriefing was not only about work but there were many fun times and social events happening. The nurses would often band together and support each other in all domains. There was an occasion on which you were going out and realised that your mesh shoes were quite dirty. The decision was made to wash the shoes and to dry them in the little bench top oven. As a child you remember your mother drying sandshoes in the oven. This proved to be a disaster as instead of having the oven on low you put it on high as you were in a hurry. On coming out of your room to check on the shoes you notice smoke billowing into the corridor. The fire brigade arrived and so one of your colleagues handed you a pair of shoes and told you to go to another floor. On descending a few flights of stairs, you peer over the balcony where you see not only the fire truck but a police car. You promptly leave the crime scene and head to the Bank night club wearing shoes that you are not sure match your dress. The burnt shoes were to remain on the oven tray in the lounge room until matron could inspect them. The nurses took a few pictures as you do. Matron inspected the shoes but not a soul provided an explanation. Later, a friend of yours tells the story of attending the switch board to cover breaks when the call came to say, 'There are shoes burning in the oven on the fourth floor of the nurses' quarters.' This story was told on many occasions, sometimes in your presence, but you would never make comment.

The end of third year nursing was approaching and for some, shift work and having a social life took a toll on the studies. During this time, you had also been struggling with an eating disorder. It was your time to knuckle down and take to the books. Time was spent doing practice exam questions in the library. The nurse educators were very supportive. At first, you would look for difficult answers instead of thinking of the basic nursing cares that you did every day. With some coaching and quality study time, you passed your final exams.

Finding Your Niche

Graduation day came and you were all in your uniforms on the stage with family and guests in the audience. There were various nursing awards given. You were not expecting an award. Your name was called out to receive the award for 'Most Improved Nurse.' At first you were embarrassed, wondering, 'How bad was I?' I never knew such a prize existed. I am not sure it did exist until then. In years to come you will look at the pottery plate that was given to you on that day and proudly reflect on the moment.

Looking back over the past three years there were many lessons learnt. It was easy to get caught up in a moment and to lose direction. It was hard work and persistence that paid off and that led to your achievement. Reflection and acceptance of constructive criticism were the key. And yes, it is ok to ask questions! One cannot expect to start out an expert, and even if you are considered an expert there is always something to learn. Although the journey thus far seems long it has only just begun!

On receiving your nursing registration in February 1984, you continue to work at the Townsville General Hospital until the middle of 1986. During this time, you meet your future husband, Ian, who is in the military. In 1986 you move to Brisbane which is just the beginning of your travels and many new nursing experiences. Travelling and working in different settings you learn that there is more than one way to skin a cat.

On moving to Brisbane, you are successful in securing a nine-month contract at a small private hospital known as St Andrew's War Memorial Hospital prior to returning to Townsville to get married. This was a different experience to working in the public system. Registered nurses were still expected to wear veils. On your first shift a colleague was asked to orientate you. It was a late shift, and you went about caring for your patients. Your colleague was chatted the next morning by the charge nurse as she had not told you to empty the bins. You were let off, but you made sure your bins were emptied from there on in. Patients had their own pharmacy supplies. Afterhours access to extra supplies initially depended on borrowed supplies. On a late shift you are busily drawing up heparin to add to the intravenous solution. You were also chatting to your colleague at the same time. Both of you sighed as you realised that the heparin had been injected into the wrong intravenous solution on your checks and balances. Both of you panic and start ringing the other wards to borrow some heparin. Much to your relief you were able to obtain an adequate supply.

In 1988, you begin your midwifery training at the Royal Brisbane and Women's Hospital. This is when you meet a lifelong friend, Pauline. It felt like you were starting your training all over again, except this time you were older, more experienced, and more confident to be assertive. It was back to ward rotations, constantly working with different colleagues and the ward reports. The difference

Finding Your Niche

this time that there was less social life and more emphasis on study. Pauline would organise study sessions for you both although you were always wanting to finish up early to get home. Some things had not changed.

The Labour Ward was a challenging experience. Each student midwife would be allocated to work with a midwife. One morning you were both allocated to care for a mother who was a primipara. The midwife spent a lot of time outside the room doing other duties as the baby was not expected to be born for some time. You stayed with the mother and completed the usual observations. To your astonishment the baby is about to crown so you alert the midwife who was just outside the door. The midwife did not come in initially as she didn't believe this could be the case. Eventually the midwife did come in, to your relief, and the baby was safely delivered. Being a student again meant that you were back to constantly proving your worth and earning the trust and respect of those with whom you were working. Some students seem to deal with his better than others. It was a long year for you and a relief to successfully finish the midwifery course.

Towards the end of your midwifery training, you found out that you were expecting your first baby and that your husband was posted to Sydney. The army accommodation that you live in is in North Ryde. When your son, Andrew was three months old you begin working at the Royal North Shore Hospital (RNSH) in the postnatal ward. Your shifts were Monday and Tuesday night shifts. Rooming in was not always the usual and many nights were spent in the nursery settling newborns. Although you continue to do some work in the Midwifery field it proves not to be your preference. After some months you decided to transfer to the casual pool at RNSH and to do agency nursing. This allowed for greater flexibility with home life and childcare. This experience enabled you to learn to adapt to many new and different situations. You had to be learning on your feet as you would arrive in a hospital with no idea of where things were and expected to take a full patient allocation. This became easier over time as you would begin to return to work in the same areas.

In 1992, you begin working as a clinical facilitator at University of Technology Sydney (UTS). You don't recall how this opportunity presented itself, but you were very excited to have been offered the opportunity to be involved in nursing education. Your first clinical practicum was at the Sydney Eye Hospital and The Sydney Hospital. It was expected that you would spend your time between the two hospitals crossing the domain to navigate between the two hospitals. This was to be the beginning of a chain of education opportunities.

In 1993, your second son, Henry, is born, and in 1994 your husband is posted to Albury Wodonga. You commenced work at the Wodonga Hospital and Albury Mercy Hospital as a casual in both general and midwifery nursing. In the same year you commence Bachelor of Nursing at LaTrobe University Albury Wodonga Campus. An opportunity presented itself to do some clinical facilitation and tutorials at the same university. The clinical placements were in rural areas such as Myrtleford and Wangaratta. This was to be your introduction to rural nursing.

During your second year of your Bachelor of Nursing, one of your subjects is Qualitative Research. You were one of five nurses that were to complete a study on farm injuries. At first you did not understand the interest but by the end of the study the reason was very clear. All nurses were working in rural settings and knew of people who have sustained a farm injury. Three of the nurses were farm wives. Farm injuries were a major community concern. The title of the study was 'A Woman's Experience When Her Husband Sustains a Farm Injury'. The research paper was written and later published.

In 1996, your husband is transferred back to Sydney where you once again work for UTS and pick up casual shifts for an agency. There was a nurse who lived across the street who came to your door to ask if you would like to do some teaching in aged care. You promptly declined the offer. Who would want to work in aged care when there are so many more attractive options? After some thought, you decide to find out more information. In 1997 the *Aged Care Act* comes into legislation. Nursing assistants were required to have education. The position was at Workskills Inc. It required writing curriculum, classroom and clinical teaching. Clinical competencies were assessed in nursing homes. Although you had little experience in aged care education, there were few nurses who did at this time. There were a variety of subjects to be taught. Most subjects were familiar, but some had to be researched. You were learning as you were teaching. This was a huge learning curve which you found very rewarding.

During your time working for Workskills, increasingly you enjoy your work. In 1998 your husband is transferred back to Townsville and you are expecting your third baby. After Lachlan was born you manage to secure casual teaching in aged care at the Great Barrier Reef Institute of TAFE and some clinical facilitation at James Cook University (JCU). In 1999 you work for the Anton Brienl Centre as a subject coordinator for a chilcare subject and an occupational therapy subject. This was to be a one-off, but it was a positive experience.

At this stage you had not worked in a hospital for about two years as you had been working in nurse education. In 1998 you commence on the casual pool at TGH. Your first shift back was to be on the Rehabilitation Ward. It would have been at least 10 years since you left TGH. There is a staff member on duty who turns to you and says, 'How ya going mate?' It was as though you had

Finding Your Niche

never left. Although you were managing working on the wards you now felt you wanted to upskill. One of your friends encourages you to complete the Transition to Practice Intensive Care Unit (ICU) programme so you rang the nurse unit manager (NUM) ICU to enquire about the details. The NUM of ICU, Pam, asked you to come in and see her. You are not sure if this is because Lachlan had turned the music up extremely loud in the background whilst you were talking and you were not sure if you had made a good first impression. Although you had not gone in with the intent to secure a job you somehow came out with one. This was to be one of the best decisions that you made. The Transition to Practice ICU programme was two years long which included two semesters at JCU in the second year. During your time completing the Transition programme, the TGH moved to Douglas and was called The Townsville Hospital (TTH). The TTH modules and the hands-on learning was second to none. There was an educator to support those on the programme as well as all had a preceptor. There were many professional and personal relationships developed which will last for years to come.

In 2003 during completion of the Transition programme you are asked to relieve in the position of Clinical Nurse Consultant Integrated Aged Care Services. This was to become your future substantive position post the Transition programme. Your studies in ICU are not wasted as the clinical knowledge would be invaluable wherever you work. One aspect of the role was completing Aged Care Assessment Team (ACAT) assessments and transitioning the frail elderly that were unable to return home to Residential Aged Care Facilities (RACFs). The other was to work within a mobile multidisciplinary geriatric team. The team was under the bed card of a Geriatrician. A mobile team meant that referrals could be made from any of the adult wards. The patients that were accepted under the bed card of the geriatrician would be the patients that would best benefit from geriatric care. The aim of the team was to prevent premature admission to RACF's and prevent deconditioning, with the aim to get patients to return home. This did not mean that nursing home type patients (NHTPs) were excluded if they could benefit from geriatric care.

Working back at TTH meant that you would reunite with some of your colleagues from your training. Moving out of ICU and working across the organisation would mean that you would get to be acquainted with a lot of other staff. There was such a friendly and collegiate feel to the atmosphere, and you really enjoy your new role.

In 2006, your father agrees to undergo heart surgery in Brisbane. You are astonished as he had previously had heart surgery in his twenties and vowed he would never go through it again. Your father and mother fly down and you join them prior to the surgery. The day of surgery was a very long day waiting for the phone call to say he was

Finding Your Niche

out of surgery and then waiting in the waiting room for the surgeon to discuss the outcome of the surgery. The surgeon tells both you and your mother that the surgery went well, and you both eagerly proceed to the ICU to see him.

On entering the ICU your mother became unsteady and lightheaded as she saw your father and the look of horror on your face. Your mother could see that your father was in trouble even without a medical background. You knew straight away that the surgeon's view of success was very different from yours. Looking at the numbers on the monitor screen, the intravenous infusions, and the balloon pump insitu, the recovery was not to be straight forward. Pauline was working at the hospital at this time who provided no end of emotional and practical support.

After almost two weeks it was time to return home and your mother would stay and be with your father. It was not long until there were further complications and you and the family returned to Brisbane to support your mother. This was a relatively short trip and once things again stabilised you returned home to work and your family. It seemed there was a loss of control over your work and personal life. Shortly after this the hospital tried to organise an interhospital transfer back to Townsville. Due to bed pressures and the inability to successfully line up a Royal Flying Doctor Service flight, this was not possible. It was at this point that your father deteriorates further.

Cyclone Larry was expected to cross the coast in North Queensland and a phone call was received for the family to gather at the hospital. It was difficult to get a flight to Brisbane, but flights were able to be organised for the next day. On arrival to the hospital the doctors explained that there was nothing more that could be done. My older brother was away and was not able to be contacted. It was a long wait through the night as family sat with your father. Not long before he passed, there was a nurse who entered the room with a telephone. The nurse had a lovely manner and facilitated the phone call from Paul to his father. The nurse stroked his head as she put the phone to his ear. It was as if he waited for the phone call to say goodbye. It was a long walk down the long, lonely corridor as we left the hospital to fly back to Townsville.

Quite a few years later, you return to the same hospital for work purposes to visit the specialised dementia unit. The NUM speaks to you, and you instantly know her voice and are sure that you have met before. At lunch it comes to you, and it was the very nurse that had facilitated Paul's phone call to your father. The nurse remembers your father, probably because he was there for a long six weeks. Nurses may not be remembered for what they look like or their name, but certainly for what they do for you. The nurses, doctors and volunteers were amazing. The long waits in the waiting room, the interhospital transfers and the fading hopes that your father comes home puts yourself in the shoes of your patients. It was tough being on the other side. These memories remain raw for a long time and the desire to ever work back in the ICU diminish. On returning to your substantive position, you know you would not want to work in any other field but elderly care.

During Cyclone Yassi in 2011, you volunteered to work at Parklands Nursing Home which is a Queensland Health facility. This made sense as you would know quite a few patients from transitioning them to Parklands from TTH. There were several other staff who had volunteered to also work through the night at Parklands and TTH with some working more than 24 hours in total. On arrival it was decided that you would work in the dementia wing. The patients were all given their evening meal, nursing care and settled for the evening. The wind gusts and rain outside gradually increased through the night. Staff tried to take turns at sleeping but most were unable to do so. Through the night, Parklands lost power and this meant the doors to the secure unit were unlocked. The Director of Nursing had her head in the power box trying to work out what had occurred, and you were right beside her. The power box was near the front doors and water had gushed in as they opened. All of a sudden you realise that the doors would be open in the dementia unit and swiftly turn around to check on the dementia patients slipping in the pooled water. Thankfully you were not injured, and no patients had left the building. It meant that patients had to be monitored even more closely overnight in case patients attempted to use the open doors to the gusty wet weather outside. Staff went to use torches, but the supply of batteries was diminished so staff were using mobile phones as torches. The power did not come back on until around breakfast time. It was a relief as the morning staff arrived on duty to take over. The nurses had handled the situation with grace and humour and still talk about this experience today. Once again nurses are banding together, this time when the community needed them the most.

Around the time of your father's passing there is a noticeable change in your voice. It was difficult to pinpoint the exact problem. It seemed to cut in and out and was difficult to maintain clear communication. Initially it was thought to be associated with grief and counselling was the recommendation although it had no impact on improving your voice. During a meeting at work a doctor recognises that you have a voice disorder. The doctor approaches you and organises a meeting as he thinks he may know what is wrong. During the meeting, the doctor tells you that one of his family members has similar problems and he organises a referral to a neurologist. It turns out that you have a disorder called spasmodic dysphonia which can only be treated with botox in Brisbane. It does not return to normal but you do see some improvement. It does become softer post-botox and you are concerned as to whether you will be able to continue to work effectively. You do work effectively and that is partially due to the support of your colleagues when needed.

Finding Your Niche

2012 saw job cuts at TTH and realignment of staff. This was a nightmare that you would never believe would happen. This was the worst part of your career. Staff across the hospital feared their jobs would be lost. The atmosphere was no longer the same while staff across the organisation wait to hear if their jobs are safe. Colleagues at your level were called into a room and were told there will be some people in this room who will lose their jobs. As staff were gradually informed of their job status there were some who had obvious physical and emotional trauma. How could anyone sack nurses?

On your way to work one morning, feeling a little overwhelmed with the realignment process, you buy a scratchie at the newsagent. Before work you began to scratch it and realise you have obviously won one of the top prizes. On a further check, you discover that you had won the top prize. It was not enough to retire but certainly changes your life and gives you more security in these uncertain times. Ian does not believe you have won the lottery so eventually comes into your work and you both confirm your winnings. It was a strange feeling as you were not as excited as you would have imagined you would have been. How could someone be excited while they or some of their colleagues have or will lose their jobs? It was not long until some of your colleagues new of your winnings. One remarking, 'Why don't you go home?' Why would I want to go home, you think to yourself? Nursing is a part of who you are. It is not about just turning up every day; it is about a commitment to your patients. The aftermark of realignment lingers for a long time and for some it will probably never be gone.

Geriatrics is a relatively young discipline compared to most. It is only recently that TTH has an Acute Care of the Elderly Ward and a Subacute Unit with beds for geriatric patients. These units were purpose built to accommodate for the special needs of this patient cohort. This meant that the mobile team would be located in the Acute Care of the Elderly (ACE) Ward on its completion. Although you stay in the same position over the years your tittle and role varies over time. Your latest tittle is CNC Acute Care of the Elderly although you are not based on the ACE ward. Your role now is mostly transitioning nursing home patients to residential care.

Transitioning patients to residential care can not only take time but can prove challenging to find a suitable placement in their current geographical location. The complexity of this has meant that some patients have relocated from Townsville. Often to physically transfer patients to these locations can be met with many barriers which has meant that staff would be instrumental in making the transfers happen. There are two occasions in particular that come to mind.

The first was when two patients were required to travel five hours north to a nursing home. Both patients had

Finding Your Niche

dementia and due to the geographical location of the nursing home the only way to directly transfer the patients was by car. You and two other nurses booked a hospital car and set out very early on the morning of the transfer with the plan to arrive at the nursing home in time for lunch. The car was packed with all the essentials that may be required to get the patients safely to their destination. Sandra and Colleen were the two other nurses on the escort. Sandra was the NUM of the ward and Colleen worked with you transitioning patients to residential care. Sandra and Colleen were in the front, and you were nominated to take the back seat with the patients. There were two stops along the way and both patients were happy to resume the journey both times although one patient did comment that he thought this was not the way home. The patient then quickly changed the subject and started to tell a story, 'I haven't been up this way for a while. I used to drive a fuel truck up this way…' This story was told repeatedly with short breaks in between. About 30 minutes from the nursing home the other patient became restless and annoyed at the story. It was a tense 30 minutes, with a big sigh of relief as we arrived at our destination. All went smoothly until this point until the three of you began to navigate the trip home.

There was lots of chatter and laughter in the car when you realise that you have taken the wrong turn back to the highway home. There was no turning back, and the range was very winding. It would add on at least another hour to the trip home. You and Sandra had been away many times together and getting lost was nothing new. Both of you took it in your stride, however Colleen was in the back and did not share the same sentiment. Eventually you are back on the main highway when another wrong turn is taken. By this time Colleen tells you both to pull over and she hails an oncoming car which you followed back to the highway to home. The rest of the trip was fairly uneventful, and all arrived home safely. It seemed that getting the patients to their destination was much easier than three nurses finding their way home.

The second escort was when one of your patients does not have relatives in Townsville and wants to transition to a nursing home in Northern NSW to be close to his nephew. This time you are on your own transferring the patient. The patient has dementia but is still able to travel by air. It is decided that you will escort the patient to the Gold Coast. Before the trip you take the time to acquaint yourself with the patient. He knows you are coming to pick him up on the day to go to the airport. On the day, he is well dressed with his suitcase in hand, waiting for the hospital bus. On disembarking from the hospital bus, he picks up your suitcase in one hand and his in the other and proceeds to where you check in. He will not take no for an answer in giving back your bag. There was a while to wait for the flight so I decide to buy coffees. The patient says, 'You do know I have dementia?' 'Yes, I do know,' you replied. After the coffee the patient clears off the rubbish and heads for the escalator. As the patient seems to be ok thus far and wanting to use the escalator, the decision is to give it a go. My goodness, he began to use the escalator as if it were a treadmill. People came to the rescue. Suitcoats, a shoe, and paperwork were in the air. On making it off the escalator both of you take a seat in the waiting lounge. The patient seemed ok, and you were grateful that he only had a small scratch considering he was on anticoagulants. The air hostess asks you both to board first. As you are showing the tickets to the flight attendant the patient walks off to take his seat. As he attempts to take his seat, he bumps his head. By this stage you are glad to be buckled up and on your way. The patient found it amusing and across the journey would be found occasionally giggling about it and telling the story.

On approaching the Gold Coast, the flight attendant asks if you would like the cherry picker to assist the patient with disembarking, which you instantly accepted. However, the cherry picker did not arrive, and the patient headed for the stairs insisting on going down. The patient descended the stairs with the flight attendant on one side and you on the other. The patient misjudged the last few steps but managed to be lowered safely to the ground. A wheelchair arrived and the patient was transferred into the care of his nephew. The nursing home later confirmed that he had arrived safely and was happily eating his dinner.

There was much reflection over this trip as to what could have been done better or differently. As a clinical nurse consultant should you have known better or been more prepared. The sight of elevators at the Gold Coast shopping centres took on a whole different meaning over the next few days. It was not until you told your story to a senior colleague that you got things in perspective. You could see the glass as either half empty or half full. The patient was now where he wanted to be, close to his family. It is often those who aren't versed in textbook theories but those who personally know the patient who will prove to be the expert.

18 years on and you are still working in geriatrics at TTH, now known as Townsville University Hospital. The accumulated nursing experience over the last forty years has laid a foundation that has contributed to you finally finding your niche in geriatrics. Nursing has not only provided an array of opportunistic and meaningful job opportunities on your travels but has allowed for many personal and professional friendships to be developed and cherished.

Nursing is a lifetime of learning, and the journey is never over. There is always something to learn or a new experience around the corner. It is those experiences and learnings that nurture and mould us to become who we are, not only as nurses, but as individuals.

Enjoy the journey!

About Desley:

Desley is a registered nurse who commenced her General Nursing Training at the Townsville General Hospital in 1981. Since completing her training Desley has relocated interstate with her family managing to work in hospitals in Queensland, NSW and Victoria in a variety of different roles.

Desley completed her Midwifery Certificate at the Royal Brisbane and Women's Hospital in 1989. In 1995 Desley completed a Bachelor of Nursing at Latrobe University Albury/Wodonga campus. During her studies in Wodonga Desley participated in a research project which was later published as 'A Woman's Experience When Her Husband Sustains a Farm Injury'. In 2003 Desley completed a Post-Graduate Certificate in Intensive Care Nursing at James Cook University Townsville Campus.

During her career, Desley has worked extensively in the education of nurses at many levels. In 1997 Desley began teaching in aged care where her passion for geriatric nursing began. After completing the Post-Graduate Certificate in 2003, Desley accepted a position as a clinical nurse consultant in gerontology at The Townsville Hospital. Over four decades of nursing Desley has worked in many different fields but finally found her niche working in geriatrics.

You can contact Desley at: djoyce37@gmail.com

CHAPTER 5

Fighting for a Calling

Kris Murphy

'A bird sitting on a tree is not afraid of the branch breaking, because its trust is not on the branch, but on its own wings.'

'Always believe in yourself.'

Charlie Wardle

I would like to dedicate this chapter to all the nursing students I have had the honour of walking alongside during their nursing studies.

Thank you for the lessons and for trusting me as you continue to make me so proud.

Hey there, Kris,

I remember you being about 14 when you first imagined becoming a nurse.

Back in the 1970s it was customary to make formal enquiries in around Year 10 regarding your anticipated career. With that in mind, following a conversation with your parents, you sent your year 10 results off with the letter you drafted to the nursing superintendent of the Princess Alexandra Hospital (PAH). Although by then you always intended on being a nurse, your father had other ideas for you, so you also applied to study teaching in order to appease him. You continued to complete your secondary school studies and did relatively well, feeling happy that you had started the process to secure your nursing future.

You selected the subjects you would study in years 11 and 12, based on the hope of a nursing career and thoroughly enjoyed biology, tolerated mathematics and were conscientious to do well in English and history. Even then, in Year 12, in 1979, you suspected you could teach whilst nursing, but not the other way around.

When you were offered a January 1980 commencement date to study nursing at the PAH, a real battle commenced between you and your father. He did and said everything in his artillery to deter you from a career in nursing and posed arguments as to why you should consider being a teacher like him. Your grandfather, uncle and aunty were also teachers and they excelled in their chosen careers. Meanwhile, you did not really know anyone who had completed their nursing studies. However, at the time you were accepted to study, you simply knew it was what you wanted to be. Interestingly, your father's youngest brother, your uncle, Ivan, was studying medicine and as he was significantly younger than your father and his other brother, your uncle, Tony, he was not much older than you. Because of this, you always felt a strong connection to Ivan, considering you both chose a career in the healthcare industry.

Your father would berate you often about your decision to do nursing in the hope that he could change your mind. He made it clear that studying teaching was a better choice for you. He had well-meaning trepidation for you as he had spoken to people who either were nurses or knew nurses and he was concerned that the shift work and unsavoury hours would take a toll on you.

You would attempt to argue your case and offset the disapproval your father projected. You argued that you were fundamentally a care giver and a nurturer and deeply cared about helping others. You reasoned that you felt you possessed a natural ability to connect with others and although you did not realise it at the time, you were an empath. You may not have explained it using those words at the time but that is at the essence of how you felt about it. You recognised from a young age that you had a natural ability to say the right thing to people when they were struggling or afraid and you felt that nursing was a 'calling' of sorts. When you thought about a career in nursing, it left you feeling satiated, almost like a thirst being quenched.

You felt certain that you were undeniably put on this earth to be a nurse and you felt energised and enthusiastic at the thought of becoming one.

You argued your case, again and again – to no avail.

However, one night, this particular battle between you and your father came to an end.

You and your father were at your grandparents' house in the upstairs lounge room and your father had spent a considerable period of time that evening arguing with you about your decision to pursue nursing as a career. You see, although he genuinely cared for you, your father was used to getting his own way and would use this tactic often during your life. Like yourself, your mother often tried to stand up for what she believed in too, however, due to sheer exhaustion would end up giving in to him by the early hours of the morning. Your father could be very manipulative and didn't like to lose an argument and never gave up trying to change any one's mind if he didn't agree with them. Through his utter determination,

Fighting for a Calling

he would invariably win all arguments as he would grind you into the ground with his tireless resolve.

On this occasion however, *you* had decided to show persistence and determination to fight for what *you* believed was right for *your* future and not give in to your father's demands. Every time your father propositioned further reasons why you should not pursue nursing as a career, you would speak up, often through anguished tears and you battled for what you knew you wanted to do the most in the world.

Eventually, after what seemed like hours of this boisterous exchange, with your father steadfastly determined to win the battle, your grandfather's voice bellowed out at your father, over your sobbing and protesting,

'FOR GOD'S SAKE PETER, LET THE GIRL DO WHAT SHE WANTS TO DO!'

The room went quiet.

You were stunned.

Your father dared not argue with your grandfather!

You finally won this battle, albeit with some help from someone you didn't expect to back you like that. But back you he did!

You and your father never discussed it again that you recall.

You started your General Nursing Training on 7th January 1980 at the PAH.

You have never looked back, Kris. Nor did you ever regret your decision to become a nurse. It was one of the best decisions you've ever made in your lifetime, and you still stand proud in being the best possible nurse today.

Act 1

Finding your first passion within nursing

Moving to Melbourne

The Alfred Hospital

Peter MacCallum Cancer Institute (your happy place)

All the way back to your beloved PAH

Kris, nursing has afforded you with so many amazing opportunities and experiences and you were always happy to put your hand up to try something different. You always felt different to many others, because you tried some pretty interesting things just to say that you had a go with no regrets.

One of these 'interesting things' was to join the army reserves whilst you were studying nursing. In second year of your nursing studies in 1981, you and your best friend joined Queensland University Regiment (QUR), as medics and completed all the mandatory, tortuous, initial employment and recruitment training that was required. You ventured to Tin Can Bay on one such occasion to complete a two-week training camp, where you met the largest mosquitoes you have ever seen in your life and (just) survived the ordeal. Your best friend to this day dislikes talking about this time, but you love teasing her about the time she almost blew herself up with a grenade.

When you were to graduate as an RN, you were offered your commission to Lieutenant, but refused it, despite them trying to convince you otherwise. They needed more women as Officers in the armed forces, however, it was at that time you knew you were heading to Melbourne to live and to be honest, the army culture and challenges posed by being female in it and the overt sexual discrimination that resulted did not make it an appealing choice.

You are to this day however, proud of accomplishing it, as it challenged you and you got to experience great team camaraderie with your fellow platoon members who were all university students at the University of Queensland (UQ).

Kris, even when you weren't the most qualified person for a position, you would never let that stop you. You would often be successful at getting a job mostly because of your sheer determination and ability to highlight your skill set in a genuine way. Having said that, you never applied for a position that you didn't think you could do, so I guess you did possess a healthy dose of self-belief most of the time. You also felt that you had your father to thank for that quality of resilience and determination. Your father definitely instilled in you that 'have a go' outlook on life. Looking back, he probably thought he was genuinely doing the right thing by you, even though it didn't always feel like it at the time. As a mother and now a grandmother yourself, you know you have not always got it right either, so it is important to you that you recognise that your father passed on some amazing gifts to you.

Ironically, you ended up landing in your nursing specialty by pure accident.

In 1985, you moved to Melbourne but did not have a job before you arrived there. At the time, you had no doubt that you would successfully land a job without too much hassle. This was back in the day before 'Key Selection Criteria' and before applying and interviewing for a position took on a life of its own.

Melbourne and regional Victoria had more than 200 public and private hospitals, quite different to Brisbane's more centralised health system at the time. So, when you arrived in Melbourne, you opened the phone book (No! There was no google back then) and went to the hospital section where they were listed in alphabetical order. You started at A and your finger landed on Alfred Hospital in Prahan. You called them on a landline telephone, explained you had newly arrived from Queensland and needed a job. The next minute, you had an interview and you were the successful candidate in an RN position on the Haematology, Oncology and Bone Marrow Transplant Unit.

Although you had garnered experience in almost every specialty during your training days at the PAH, you were never placed on the Haematology Oncology Ward. This was a highly specialised area of nursing and you could honestly tell some horror stories of what you were exposed to as a novice without adequate training. Today, there is so much mandatory training to become a haematology oncology nurse and administer chemotherapeutic agents to very unwell, immunosuppressed patients with complex needs. You have to complete additional study and ensure you adhere to strict safe handling practice. You have since completed all this training, but here you were in the 1980s, working in this specialty ward without any formal training.

It would never be acceptable in this day and age.

You survived, and so did the patients in your care and you quickly fell hopelessly in love with this area of nursing.

It was intimate and complex, sometimes dangerous and often chaotic, evoking feelings that you had never experienced before. Caring for people who are fighting for their life every day afforded you the opportunity to really connect on another level with them. They became really important to you, and you got to know them and their nearest and dearest intricately, as treatments were long and repetitive. You loved how they trusted you, and you felt worthwhile and developed a sense of making a real difference in nursing these patients.

You would celebrate their triumphs in achieving remission from their leukaemia and watched on at the joy that brought them and their loved ones.

Alternatively, you have held the hand of dying patients as they took their last breath.

Many times.

You would go into your shift early or stay late to sit with patients who did not have close family with them to bring them some additional comfort.

You would work with the clinical team to save a patient's life when they went into septic shock after their immunosuppressed bodies surrendered to a bacterial infection.

Fighting for a Calling

It seemed cruel at times what you were doing to them, but the alternative was not on their radar, and they made an informed choice to fight hard for their lives.

You were in awe of these patients and remain so today.

It is true what they say: that you do not realise how resilient you are until you have to be! You witnessed countless examples of this during your 30-plus years as a haematology oncology nurse.

Because you now recognised that this was the type of nursing you wanted to specialise in, when a position was advertised at the renowned Peter MacCallum Cancer Institute to complete the post graduate chemotherapy nursing course, you went for it. You remember a comment being made to you when being interviewed for the position saying you did not have a lot of experience in this field of nursing (at that stage approximately 12 to 18 months only), to which you replied, 'But how am I going to get the experience you need me to have if I don't get given the chance to get it?'

You got the job!

You were one of only three RNs chosen for the position and you were so delighted the day you found out.

You honestly believe that if you didn't speak up and say that and other comments about your personal attributes and your never-give-up attitude, you would not have been successful. The position gave you access to the chemotherapy nursing course and then you remained on as staff working in the Day Oncology Unit. This was the beginning of one of the happiest working experiences of your life. You commenced the Chemotherapy Nursing Course shortly afterwards with two other ladies, whom you developed a close bond with, and you stayed working at Peter MacCallum Cancer Institute until you returned to Queensland over six years later. It was definitely your happy place and you worked with a dynamic and cohesive team during that time and until this day, it was the happiest work environment you ever worked in.

Your career in haematology oncology nursing spanned over 34 years. You worked in the public, private and not-for-profit sectors, including at The Leukaemia Foundation and The Cancer Council. You got to present papers at Domestic and International Conferences, become a CVAD specialist and Apheresis Coordinator and teach these skills to other nurses. You helped develop and update resources used Australia wide for patients and nursing staff and chaired working groups and committees and facilitated workshops for healthcare professionals and patients. You played a role in new innovative approaches in the delivery of healthcare and designed teaching tools that assisted other nurses to support their patients to get the information they needed to understand their condition.

You also came full circle and a year after joining Queensland Health in 2012, found yourself back at the PAH working in their Day Oncology Unit as a clinical nurse. You then ventured into the subspecialty of Stem Cell Collection and studied Apheresis Nursing and was successful in becoming Cancer Service's Apheresis Coordinator. This role saw you branch out into the Quality Management side of the unit and you were instrumental in its success in gaining National Association of Testing Authorities (NATA) reaccreditation. A huge undertaking and a very satisfying learning opportunity that helped secure your next big role in patient safety, quality and innovation at a different health service.

You learned that nurses don't just perform clinical tasks, assess and plan nursing care and keep patients safe from harm, but their role is much more diverse. Nurses are also innovators in healthcare and advocate for their patients. They encourage the delivery of evidence based best practice, health promotion, educate the public, run hospitals, sit on the Board of Directors, investigate clinical incidents and facilitate improvement, teach at universities and assist in healthcare professional training.

Nurses are leaders and role models.

You now encourage student nurses and new grads to find their passion within nursing. There may be more than one! Follow your passion and learn and experience all that your newfound passion affords you. It keeps things interesting and ensures longevity in your nursing career.

For yourself, on reflection, you never realised how many diverse opportunities you would experience when selecting haematology oncology as your chosen passion in nursing and until only a few years ago, you continued to work in this field until you decided that it was now time to take a leap of faith and try a new direction.

Act 2

What they didn't tell you about a career in nursing

The bullying culture in nursing and how to navigate it

The painful moments within your career and how you grew from them
How you handled it
How you should have handled it

WARNING: *The content in this section makes reference to suicidal ideation and the descriptions may be triggering for some readers.*

Although a sensitive topic, you make no apologies for going into detail, as it is important to you that the reader understands how serious this behaviour is in any occupation and hopes the

Fighting for a Calling

reader can learn some strategies on how to protect themselves from it. You also hope by writing your story that others may also recognise what behaviours constitute bullying and understand the detrimental consequences for the victim.

> *'And once the storm is over, you won't remember how you made it through, how you managed to survive. You won't even be sure, whether the storm is really over. But one thing is certain. When you come out of the storm, you won't be the same person who walked in. That's what this storm's all about.'*
> Haruki Murakami

Kris, you have always simply refused to cut corners when delivering healthcare to sick, vulnerable patients.

In 1983, even as a new graduate, you understood the essence of what we now call 'person-centred care'. You would often see some other nurses take the easy way out, not follow best practice, display laziness, not team focused, had terrible approaches when it came to patient interaction, and you really had difficulty understanding these attitudes in such a caring profession.

It challenged you so much.
You found it very confronting.
You still do.

Kris, anyone who knows you well will attest to the fact that you are immensely proud to be a nurse and you take your role very seriously. Don't get me wrong, you still have fun at work too, however, you are happiest when working alongside a great team who support and encourage one another, even on the busiest of shifts. You like to have fun with the patients, too, and use humour appropriately, and you always did have a natural ability to make them feel safe and listened to.

You often feel, however, that you sometimes make things harder for yourself in your working life as a nurse due to your deeply embedded core values of integrity, diligence, discipline, honesty and responsibility. Coupled with your strong work ethic, some of the most challenging periods of your career have occurred when your values were being challenged or undermined. Because you are conscientious and help others and go the extra mile for your patients, you have opened yourself up to judgement from others who choose not to act professionally. You get judged a lot in your day to day working life, even to this day. You are also very intuitive and can pick up a negative vibe very easily. Being an empath also makes you an easy target that other people can take advantage of.

It is time to share with the reader some of the most challenging times in your nursing career that brought you to your knees. It's true what they say: 'What doesn't kill you makes you stronger.'

Fighting for a Calling

You are a living testament to this.

To those reading this, particularly student nurses; If there is one thing you take from this story, I really want you to learn and understand that there *is* a better way to manage certain situations you may find yourself in to ensure your overall psychological safety at work is preserved and to also maintain your self-respect in the process.

If there is one thing you wish you were more prepared for in a nursing career, it is the reality that not all nurses are nice. The phrase that is often used is 'nurses eat their young'. Isn't that horrible and baffling at the same time? But, in your personal experience, the phrase rings true. You only wish that you had a book like this to read or a clinical facilitator like you to guide and educate your younger self through the pitfalls of working within a discipline that is female dominated. Someone to impart wisdom of lessons learned to empower you to arm yourself with knowledge about people who bully and how Graded Assertiveness is a very powerful tool in your artillery.

By now, Kris, you have been bullied several times in the workplace. I want to tell the reader about two of these occasions, the last being the most vile and horrendous experience that you thought you would die.

You learned that you did not possess the necessary skills and tools when you had your experiences with workplace bullying, but now you do. You also had to face the uncomfortable reality that *you* also played a role in these shocking situations. Your response to the bullying made the situation worse. Your emotions and debilitating anxiety, which in turn provoked rumination and catastrophising, made the ordeal a living hell.

Bullying is an ongoing or repeated misuse of power, with the intention to cause deliberate psychological harm. It is repeated and unreasonable behaviour directed towards a person that creates a risk to their health or safety.

Bullying behaviours can be verbal, physical, covert, cyberbullying and social.

Behaviours that are exhibited by those who bully include (not an exhaustive list):

- *Behaving in an unpleasant way towards or near someone*
- *Giving nasty looks, eye rolling, name calling, rude comments, being impolite repeatedly*
- *Spreading rumours or untruths about a person or misrepresenting a person*
- *Constant negative comments directed at a person*
- *Ignoring a person on purpose or refusing to engage with them*
- *Harassing a person based on their weight, race, religion, gender or sexual orientation*

- *Misappropriating your position of power over another person*[ix]

The very first time it happened to you, it was so overt and targeted, that you could barely fathom it to be happening. You had worked at the hospital for several years already but had been successful at securing another RN position when they opened up a new specialty unit. In the end you resigned as you just could not handle the day-to-day behaviour exhibited towards you and would spend countless hours staying up to the early hours of the morning ruminating over the events of each day. In your previous part time role at the same hospital, you had experienced healthy working relationships with the people you engaged with hospital wide as your role required you to attend just about every department within it to perform your role.

You were good at relationship building and reading people and would adjust yourself at times to accommodate difficult personalities in order to 'get the job done' and maintain healthy working relationships. You did explain to your manager at the time exactly what happened to you on a daily basis when working alone with the bully in the unit, however, she was friendly with this person, who happened to be my senior in a clinical nurse role and although my manager did not condone the behaviour nothing was done to stop it.

However, when you took matters into your own hands and decided to leave the toxic environment to protect yourself from further harm, you were brave enough before you left and spoke to this person face to face. You wanted to speak up for yourself and have an opportunity to tell her the effect her behaviour had on you. During that conversation, the person simply said, 'I just don't like you and when I don't like a person this is how I am with them. It's a problem I have but I can't help it.'

Yeah! You were gobsmacked.

She could see how her behaviour was affecting you, but she showed zero empathy towards you and justified the behaviour because she 'just didn't like you'.

The mistake you made at the time, is you kept looking at yourself as the problem and that you must be doing something wrong for people to treat you this way.

The only mistake you made, Kris, was in how you responded to the bullying.

You tried too hard to please them.
You bent over backwards to do things that you thought would please them in order for them to 'like' you and treat you better.
You did not use graded assertiveness to manage the conflict and have difficult conversations.

Fighting for a Calling

Instead, you came from a place of 'emotion mind' when speaking to the bully and you now know that whenever you speak whilst in 'emotion mind', it never ends well.

One thing you have now learned is that bullies love it when you try harder to please them. It's like they get off on it. But whilst you are bending over backwards trying to please them, they are quietly just laughing at you and thinking how pathetic you are. It does not help you or the situation, in fact it makes it work. Any self-respect you may have had has gone out the window.

This was you!

Oh, Kris, how devastating that you did this to yourself in order to fix this problem. And so, so sad and pathetic too. Harsh? Maybe! But you eventually figured it out just before it was too late.

Interestingly, many years after this first case of bullying, you found yourself face to face with this person when attending an education day. She approached you to introduce herself and shake your hand and you just looked at her unbelievably and in a shocked state, indicated that you had previously worked together. You could not comprehend how a person who had made you doubt yourself so much and caused you so much pain, was completely unaware of you in that moment.

You had another encounter of bullying many years later with a person who was in a position of power over you. Your working relationship with this person started out wonderfully, but years later when you began to speak up when they made derogatory comments about patients and used racist undertones towards indigenous patients, you basically put a target on your back. These comments and the associated behaviour in meetings challenged your core values and you firmly believed that it was your duty to always respect and protect others, especially those that were vulnerable. These were your non-negotiables in life, and social justice and human rights are very dear to your heart. Institutional racism exists in this country because people don't take a stand. With you, however, the lioness would arise, and you would stand proud and articulately say it was 'not ok' to speak like that. Your punishment for your crime was to contend with relentless micromanagement in the role that you knew backwards and excelled in and all of a sudden, nothing you did was good enough.

This is exactly why nurses don't report bullying. They feel powerless that they doubt that they will get the support they need, and they really don't know who to trust, as the perpetrator usually has a 'band of buddies' willing to support them, so the buddies don't end up on the receiving end of their behaviour also.

But you survived.

Fighting for a Calling

Chasing more roles on your career bucket list and landing your dream job, you eventually left the PAH in 2017, to take on a highly coveted role. You had worked tirelessly for over a year preparing for such a role. You were working at the PAH in a training position for the Digital Hospital rollout which put PAH at the forefront of healthcare innovation and technology. You would head to the library after work most days including weekends and study for hours each day. You watched and waited and knew these roles were advertised very rarely and that if you were to be successful in finding this position it would be at an emerging or expanding health service. You knew this particular health service was expanding and building a tertiary, state of the art facility and you had it firmly within your sights.

You saw the ad and applied for the position. You made it to interview where you had to deliver a presentation to four panel members. The interview could not have gone better, and you seemed to find every bit of courage that day and you nailed it.

A few days after the interview, one of the panel members, soon to be in a position of power over you, asked if you would meet her before they made the final decision. Looking back, the signs were staring you in the face at that meeting. This person sat opposite you but positioned her body sideways and looked away from you the entire time. She would barely look at you. You were so puzzled by her behaviour and thought at the time how unprofessional it was. Eager to impress her, you answered all her questions and tried to ignore her glaringly obvious poor behaviour towards you.

You then got the phone call to offer you the job! In that moment, you were so full of pride that you had achieved a career goal. You moved your whole life and were ready to embrace another steep learning curve to succeed in your role in your 'dream' job.

Then the worst thing happened to you.

You entered a very dark and terrifying time after experiencing the absolute cruellest, most severe, constant and calculated workplace intimidation and bullying. The perpetrator was well known to the role of bully and had successfully pushed many people to leave their role over the preceding eight years, prior to yourself, in order to satisfy their own personal agenda. They may have had a friend who needed a job and they wanted them in a role, or they just didn't like you and wanted you gone.

You would either be treated badly or ignored completely by this person and sometimes yelled out in front of the team. When you looked around for help, everyone had their heads down pretending to type on their computers because no one was brave enough to speak up or protect you. They did not want to be you! Two of your closest colleagues, who have also now left this environment, would be your voice of reason. They would confirm that the treatment towards you was abhorrent, but they could not go with you to support reporting it as at the time neither had a permanent position. They feared losing their jobs if they spoke up, since each was responsible for supporting their family.

That is the power the bully had.
My colleagues would end up with a target on their backs if they dared help me.

This was a place you had been twice before and faced with it again, you felt so pathetic and weak and scared and vulnerable. You still did not have the necessary skills to manage this behaviour and resorted to your previous way of dealing with it by trying harder and working harder and you thought every day, 'If only I can be good enough, they will see I am worthy.' This time however, so embarrassed were you that you had once again fallen victim to this unrelenting and soul-destroying behaviour, you decided to tell no-one.

Not your closest friends.
Not your children.
Not your seniors at work.

You feared you would be judged.
You also did not trust anyone by this point.

It was a lonely and desolate place to be, Kris.

Because it had happened to you before, you were scared that anyone you did tell would think there was something wrong with you and that you had caused the problem. You lived on your own, too, and you were working ridiculous hours to compensate for the inadequacies you perceived in yourself as a direct influence of what the bully was saying to you on a daily basis. Towards the end, you even went into work all day every weekend to try and be so organised that the bully would back off a bit during the working week.

However, one afternoon you drove into your garage, turned off the car and just sat there for what seemed like hours. On the trip home each evening for months, you had constant thoughts to drive really fast into a power pole. But you didn't, because you could see your children having to deal with the aftermath of the decision. Not you.

Kris, I am not bringing this all up to be dramatic, or to somehow make people feel sorry for you, but simply because I want people to know and understand the devastating effects of being bullied.

It is the *blackest* of *black*.
It is *hopeless*.
You feel defeated and unworthy.
It is wanting your life to end.
It is not seeing a solution.

Fighting for a Calling

That night, you decided that the best solution for you and your children was to end your life.

You made a plan.

You put your affairs in order systematically, to ensure that when it was all over, the children would have clear instructions of your wishes for them, and you knew that they would be ok financially because of your life insurance and superannuation cover.

It was a huge relief, really.

However, it was after a night of getting no sleep and not being in a good state of mind that one of the only work colleagues you trusted, checked in on you and you alluded to something concerning in your reply. You can barely remember what it was now, because you were in such a bad space. Your colleague was so concerned she alerted your son and set in motion a series of events that finally got you the help you so desperately needed. You were initially angry at your colleague but, Kris, you would have done the same thing if you were in your colleague's position. You know she just wanted you safe.

The good news that came out of this life changing moment, despite confronting for them, is that your children finally knew the burden you were carrying, and they could be there to help you through it. You were also admitted to a private treatment facility to keep you safe and you got the help you needed to recover from the trauma of the bullying. You were able to tell your best friend, too, and slowly try and allow others to give you support. Sometimes today, you still struggle with feeling you have to do everything yourself, but you have learned that being vulnerable and asking for support is necessary. People are not mind readers. You have to tell them what you need.

Surprisingly, some people were not as supportive as you thought they would be, and you really learnt who your true friends were at that time. Then, on the other hand, people who were more acquaintances were the most thoughtful and caring and turned up to show their love and support. They remain very dear to you to this day.

It was in that treatment facility that you were introduced to the abundance of learning you would embark on and to say it has been life changing would be an understatement.

You are now better equipped than ever to deal with toxic behaviour in the workplace and you have learned that it is their problem, not yours.

You have also learned how to phrase your words in times of potential conflict to elicit a better outcome.

You also know and understand that all you need to do is role model exemplary, professional behaviour and use graded assertiveness when needing to express genuine concern and maintain your self-respect.

Fighting for a Calling

You now impart this newfound knowledge and skills to your students if they find themselves in difficult situations with other nursing staff while on clinical placement. They get to practice these well-founded strategies, using graded assertiveness and conflict resolution techniques, and then observe the positive way the situation turns around in their favour.

It preserves working relationships, empowers the students and maintains their self-respect during the process.

In the end, you became grateful for the last bullying experience, as it set you on a different trajectory in managing those nurses who are not kind. It still makes you sad and unhappy at times and you still are challenged by ongoing anxiety as a consequence of the trauma, but now you no longer allow other people's behaviour to affect you and your happiness at work.

Act 3

The great stuff
Your second calling

Taking a leap of faith to follow my other passion and play a role in shaping our future nurses

Using your personal experiences and transferable skills in my nursing specialty and patient safety to impart knowledge to future nurses

Sharing lessons learned with nursing students to protect them from the pitfalls of the nursing occupation

> 'Kindness makes you the most beautiful person, no matter what you look like.'
> Anonymous

This is the part of your story, Kris, where you finally realise another dream.
You become a teacher after all!

During your 38-plus years as a registered nurse, one of your most fulfilling roles was teaching other health professionals to acquire new knowledge and skills. To assist others to learn and to experience innovative

Fighting for a Calling

approaches to healthcare provision gives you an enormous amount of satisfaction. To assist them to open themselves to accept change that improves patient safety and delivers evidence based, best practice, quality healthcare is a career highlight.

Healthcare professionals, including medical officers, allied health and nursing staff, are mostly used to being in control and knowing what they are doing. Many of them feel really uncomfortable when they do not know something or need to learn about something that may put them outside their comfort zone.

Over many years, you have experienced first-hand what happens to health professionals when they don't feel in control.

Well, actually, one of two things happen.

They either surrender, put their hands up and admit they do not have a clue what to do, welcoming your support and direction in the learning environment, or they deflect and swerve and fight the learning process, scared that they will lose face.

It is an interesting phenomenon, and you have witnessed some incredibly poor behaviour with the latter. You yourself have always embraced change and you do struggle to understand the resistance of nurses to embrace it when it invariably means improved processes, safer care delivery and improved efficiency in the service.

You do also love a challenge, remember? You predominantly try genuinely hard to instil a level of safety and understanding in the learning environment, so participants feel comfortable to relinquish their control and trust you in their learning process. Some of your own personal learning experiences that have been the most enjoyable, was when the clinical trainer/educator has explained things in a way that made sense and they were patient and listened to your questions or concerns. It is your experience too that some trainers forget that this information is brand new and people usually take a bit of time to grasp it. You don't know what you don't know!

A great example of this was the Integrated Electronic Medical Record (ieMR) rollout.

You were part of the Queensland Health (QH) clinical training team across three separate Hospital and Health Services (HHS), to deliver training to thousands of health professionals to navigate an electronic medical record and documentation system. Depending on the specialty in which they worked was contingent on what application you taught, and you soon realised that you were able to grasp this new concept quite easily and this digital hospital gig was right up your alley. During your time training clinicians across Metro South HHS, Gold Coast Health and Sunshine Coast HHS, you realised that teaching was embedded in your genes.

You received an abundance of positive feedback from participants and the best feedback in your opinion was that you made them feel comfortable whilst learning. So, you made a decision that you wanted more of this teaching in nursing gig and pivoted towards roles in clinical facilitation (CF).

You have had countless years of experience teaching postgraduate health professionals in the clinical setting, but you now wanted to play a role in shaping the future nurses of today.

You now work as a CF for QUT and USC and support the learning of nursing science undergraduate students whilst on clinical placement. The rewards you have received since commencing this role in 2019 has been immeasurable. You pride yourself on being a nurturing facilitator, ensuring the students feels safe and you also expend a lot of energy settling their nerves at the commencement of placement, resulting in them achieving their best performance.

In addition to your CF role, you now also teach Nursing Science undergraduates at the University of the Sunshine Coast (USC). Second year students in Ethics and Law in Healthcare and Graduate Entry students in Introduction to Nursing Practice. Not only do nurses today have to be adequately prepared for care provision in an ever-increasing complex healthcare system and diverse patient population, but they are called upon to show leadership skills as part of their role.

Every group of students you have met and have had the privilege of walking alongside have taught you some lessons also. You have reflected on your past adversity and ensure you offer a guiding hand to steer student nurses towards the correct way to manage conflict in the workplace. You help them find their voice so they can become empowered and speak up in the interests of patient safety. Nothing makes you prouder and more satisfied than to witness a student who was initially struggling with their self-esteem, to grow and learn how to adopt a different perspective that affords them positive reward and recognition. They are then able to demonstrate their adherence to the seven Nursing and Midwifery Board of Australia (NMBA) Standards and be well on their way to becoming an RN.

You will never take this responsibility for granted.

To have played a small role in shaping the practice and ultimate success of our future nurses is a role that you hold dear to your heart and you hope you continue to be energised and humbled by its importance.

Fighting for a Calling

About Kris:

Kris is a registered nurse, clinical facilitator, educator and sessional academic who completed her nursing studies at the Princess Alexandra Hospital in Brisbane in 1983. Kris 'fell' into her specialty in nursing, Haematology Oncology and Apheresis nursing by accident when living in Melbourne. However, she adored every element of it and found her first passion within nursing. This afforded her well over 35 years of immense joy, many challenges and heartache along with personal and professional achievements across a variety of settings. The patients she has met and nursed along the way and their beloved friends and family have inspired her to personally show courage in the most challenging of times.

They are her heroes!

Kris is also a mother of two to Thomas and Emily and she believes this to be her greatest achievement in life. Her little granddaughter, Ayla, was born in 2020 and a new level of love was born.

Awarded the Pride of Workmanship award, Kris feels strongly about patient advocacy. She still works clinically and teaches Health, Law and Ethics and Introduction to Nursing Practice at USC. Kris also advocates fiercely for her students and sees her other role as a clinical facilitator and educator as her second passion within her successful nursing career.

Kris believes it is the ultimate privilege to play a small role in shaping our future nurses. She is unapologetically proud to be a nurse and has always been humbled by the unique opportunities it has afforded her and the valuable learning along the way.

You can contact Kris at: k.murphy62@bigpond.com

CHAPTER 6

To Be a Nurse

Jackie Morgan

I dedicate this chapter to the mentors who have helped me develop into the nurse I am today, assisting me in following my passion for cancer nursing. Although there are many, these people have had the most significant impact on me professionally. These people have gone above and beyond to share their knowledge and skills, support my career development over many years, and been there when I needed that extra bit of encouragement to keep going.

To Sue Forster (RIP), Dr Robert Hitchins and Brian Amos, from the bottom of my heart, thank you for the time and effort you put into helping me over many years. Your efforts never went unnoticed and have been appreciated. Because you invested time in me, I realised how vital mentoring others is and I have tried hard to pass this on to the next generation of nurses. The results of your efforts have not just helped me, but ultimately, it has improved the quality of patient care myself and others have given over many years.

Introduction

I always wanted to be a nurse from the time I was four years old when my aunt and uncle gave me a nurse's kit. From that time on, I had decided that nursing is what I wanted to do and chose all my subjects at high school accordingly. I even joined the junior Red Cross when I was about 10 years old to learn about nursing and volunteered in a local nursing home. When I applied to several hospitals to enter nurses training, I was offered placement in three hospitals in Queensland. I chose the hospital that was closest to my home, the Gold Coast Hospital. The year I started was 1983, and at that time, student nurses required to live in the nurses' quarters for at least the first year. I assume this was the matron's way of keeping an eye on us and ensuring we focused more on our studies and less on other external distractions.

Reflecting on nursing from the early 1980's seems like a lifetime ago in some ways, yet in other ways, not so long at all. Living in the nurses' quarters was so much fun. Of course, we broke the curfews and a few rules as we went out to the nightclubs and many nurses brought their boyfriends in for the night. I loved living there, and made some great friends too. It helped us bond as a training group, and we often studied together leading up to our exams or doing assignments. This chapter is my letter to myself at this young age when starting as a nurse. In these words, there is some of the information... I wish I had known or realised earlier to make the journey just that little bit easier. I hope some nurses, especially those just starting out, read this chapter and the whole book and find some pieces of information or advice that may assist them as they learn and grow as a nurse.

Nursing training

In January 1983, just one week before I turned 17, I began my three-year hospital-based nursing training at the Gold Coast Hospital. I loved every minute of it. Working shift-work full-time and studying simultaneously was hard work, but my new world was like a great adventure to me at the time. I was learning new things every day, and I discovered that I loved caring for sick people. There was so much to learn: anatomy and physiology, diseases, medications and side effects, nursing care, good communication skills, being organised and planning care well. The learning and assessment requirements seemed endless at the time. I developed new and lasting friendships, was mentored by some amazing nurses, and found my new direction in life.

Dear Jackie,

Congratulations, you have made your dream come true! You studied at school, focused on the subjects you needed to get into nursing, and you did it. You made it happen! Now you have a new challenge – completing your nursing training. Completing your training won't be easy, but you will do quite well if you work hard and focus. Keeping up with study whilst working full-time requires organisation, commitment, and discipline. For you, this will come quite easily, as you will enjoy being a nurse. Throughout this training period you will be fortunate to have one of the most incredible nurse educators, Sue Forster and her team to teach, guide and encourage you. Sue was an ex-army nurse who was extremely intelligent and loved teaching young nurses.

(For those nurses who trained at the old Gold Coast Hospital, I am sure there are many who reflect on Sue's input into the early development of their careers with appreciation for her dedication).

Your biggest distraction will be your new friends and colleagues in the nurses' quarters. Being allowed to go out and drink with friends with no one to check on your curfew time will be fun but potentially a trap if you don't spend enough time studying. You will get your driver's licence and your first car – a 1965 Hillman Super Minx, Mark IV. You will find that this freedom brings you so much fun. You also need to be careful; your generation doesn't yet understand the dangers of drink driving. Whilst working in the emergency department, you will see just how dangerous the combination of drinking and driving can be, especially with the improvements and speed capabilities of cars in the decades to come.

Learning and finding your way is fun and such a special time. Don't take it for granted, but rather embrace it. During this time, you will set the scene for your ongoing career in nursing. You will meet some of the most extraordinary, inspiring, and caring nurses who become role models and mentors to you and others around you. Working with these people will help you enormously as you continue in your nursing career. Think back on them often when you face difficult decisions. What might they do in your current situation? The knowledge and experiences they share with you will be crucial for your future. Your challenge once you have qualified will be to be an inspirational nurse to other new nurses. You will learn to do that and be an inspiration to many in the years to come.

Cancer nursing

Some nurses find it challenging to choose a specific area of nursing to work in, but this will happen quite quickly for you. Observing some inadequacies in care for cancer patients as you were training, you will soon set off on a path to learn more about caring for cancer patients. At only 21 years of age, you have no idea the journey that decision will lead you on. Your quick decision to enrol in the postgraduate course in cancer nursing will serve you well. Once again, during this cancer nursing training, you will meet some more great mentors and colleagues who will also be friends for life.

Cancer care seems to draw a particular type of person who is comfortable being with patients during the most challenging times in their lives. You will soon have a chance encounter with one of the most intelligent and kind humans you have ever known. Dr Robert Hitchins will teach you so much about cancer, chemotherapy and, most importantly, about communicating well with cancer patients and their loved ones. Following his example, you too will learn to be with people when they hear for the first time that they have cancer, need chemotherapy, have incurable cancer, and when told they only have months, weeks or days to live. Cancer nursing will soon become your passion which lasts for your entire career.

To Be a Nurse

Over the next 30-plus years you will observe many changes in the field of cancer nursing. The number of chemotherapy drugs which will be developed throughout your career as a nurse could not be imagined from where you first started. You will see the introduction of a new class of anti-emetics which will revolutionise patients' experience with chemotherapy. Now, chemotherapy is so much more tolerable, and the stories people used to hear of people vomiting for days after treatment are a much rarer occurrence since the discovery of these drugs. You will see the first immunotherapy drug, Mabthera, introduced in the early 1990s to treat lymphomas. This will be one of the greatest breakthroughs in cancer treatment in many years. The discovery of many more of these types of drugs will follow, and become available in the years to come to treat almost every type of cancer.

The cancer nursing workforce will grow rapidly during your time in nursing, from a new specialty in healthcare to a much larger group with major cancer treatment centres in public and private hospitals all over Australia. During these early years, you, Brian Amos from the Queensland Cancer Fund and the committee from the Gold Coast Oncology Nurses Group will organise and deliver several cancer nursing courses over six weeks each. You will develop your confidence in public speaking and your passion for educating other nurses. This time of collaboration with Brian and the Oncology Nurses Group committee and members will be one of the most empowering and motivating in your career. Opportunities like this, where there is so much support and enthusiasm for developing a new specialty in nursing are rare. With Brian's never-ending motivation and energy and Dr Rob's continuous commitment to assist you to develop cancer nurses' knowledge and expertise on the Gold Coast, you will form a great team to get the job done!

The funny moments

Having a great sense of humour myself, I was pleased to find funny moments happen in nursing. There are things I look back on now, and they still crack me up laughing. I clearly remember the day an elderly gentleman with dementia escaped from a medical ward when I was a student nurse. I heard another patient yell out desperately, 'He's going to jump,' so I ran towards where she was pointing, to see this man half-standing, holding onto a pole on a railing. Before anyone could get to him, he jumped off the railing and yelled out as he disappeared from my sight, 'Bombs away…' The drop to the ground was about six feet. He was uninjured and caught quickly by some staff. However, every time I think of this incident that could have led to quite significant harm, I still laugh at the vision of him yelling out, 'Bombs away…' as he jumped.

Amidst the seriousness of nursing, you will find some hilarious moments that only those who work in healthcare can appreciate. These moments are the moments that keep you and your colleagues going on tough days. You will develop what they call a 'nurses' humour', an ability to find something humorous in a serious situation. It's essential to learn to enjoy these moments as they are a great stress relief when you are nursing. Sharing some funny moments at work can be the moments that help to build a good team, so bring your sense of humour to work, and when it's the right time, share some fun with your colleagues.

You will find that patients also like to have humour around them at the right times. Humour can help in building relationships with patients. Over the years, you will learn how to integrate humour into your nurse's toolkit of skills and learn to use it to break the ice between you and your patients and their carers. Patients seem to appreciate someone with a great sense of humour and a friendly smile. Make sure you smile regularly at work and try to create that positive environment. It will help put people at ease and may also help them laugh and focus away from their problems, even for just a moment. In the proper context, humour can help everyone to have a better day.

Advances in nursing

When I started nursing in 1983, computers were only in the early stages of development and were not used in the hospital. We typed our assignments on typewriters, going over our mistakes with white out. There was no cut and paste and no internet to search for information. We spent a lot of time in the hospital library, trawling through journal articles and books and seeking assistance from our fantastic librarians. It was in the late 1980s when computers were introduced into the hospital with some basic programmes. However, it would be another couple of decades before electronic health records were introduced. In the meantime, we worked with paper charts delivered to us by the medical records department and hospital volunteers. It was about the same time that mobile phones became available. Dr Hitchins was the first person I knew who purchased a mobile phone. It was the size of a brick (an exaggeration) and it took a couple of decades before mobile phones became much smaller and more user friendly.

You can never be prepared for the advances that will happen in your lifetime, from computers and the internet to mobile phones, laptops and iPads. You will see the introduction of electronic health records, robotic surgery, online results, email communication, and so much more in terms of technology at work. Nursing specialties will develop, bringing fantastic new opportunities for nurses to further expand their knowledge and skills and follow their interests throughout their careers. The old white dress uniform with white shoes will soon be a thing of the past, allowing for more comfortable uniforms such as callouts, shorts, long pants and eventually scrubs. The old terms 'Matron' and 'Sister' will soon be gone, and patients and colleagues will instead call each other by their first names.

In cancer care, you will see the introduction of new and improved drugs to treat cancer and manage side effects. You will see improved anti-nausea medications, numerous new chemotherapy drugs, and a new form of treatment that will revolutionise cancer care, immunotherapy. Cancers previously untreatable with chemotherapy, such as melanoma and prostate cancer, will soon be offered treatment. Infusions will soon be administered through pumps and gone will be the days of counting drip rates to administer them; every infusion will be administered via a pump. Many more changes will soon be made to improve patient safety. These changes will be necessary, but at times they may seem overwhelming. Hang in there and focus on one challenge at a time. Remember, if you feel overwhelmed, it is likely that some of your colleagues are feeling this way too. Work together, support each other through it and before long, you will master so many more skills and teach others. Change will be a constant throughout your career.

Nursing training will soon transfer to universities, and nursing will be regarded as a profession with pay rates increasing accordingly. You will need to adapt to a whole new world of technology, advancing knowledge, new clinical skills, a focus on quality and safety, a changed hierarchical system in healthcare, financial accountability and so much more. Nurses involvement in research will expand during this time. You will see the increasing emergence of specialist nursing roles including nurse practitioners. You will be involved in developing clinical pathways for chemotherapy treatments and gain an increased awareness of the need for evidence-based practice.

There are many nurses who have since retired, or are close to retiring, who fought hard for the benefits and opportunities you will soon be enjoying. Don't ever take for granted the efforts of those nurses who have gone before you to pave the way for where your profession is now. Take some time to reflect occasionally on the sacrifices and efforts of those nurses.

Bullying

Although bullying has been present throughout all cultures, societies, races, organisations and workplaces for many years, I still find it surprising that there is so much bullying in nursing. How can this be in a profession that cares for others and understands the importance of compassion and encouragement? I'm not sure we will ever know the answer to this question, but I and many others will be severely affected by bullying at some stage of their career. One of my early educators and mentors, Sue Forster, wrote a great book on bullying, *Do you want bullying with that?*[x].

Throughout your career, there will be bullies who will try to make you feel insignificant and unworthy. Most likely, some will succeed. You will need to develop some resilience and stamina to withstand the effects of bullies you will encounter throughout your career. There will be times when you won't succeed, and you will be affected. You will suffer the personal effects of bullying, such as high stress levels, insomnia and depression. I wish there were some way of protecting you and others from bullies but, unfortunately, it requires life experience and developing skills to become more resilient to able to withstand their bullying actions. Even with these skills, you and many other nurses will still be bullied, most often by senior nurses and nurse managers.

One of the best ways to stop bullying (as suggested by Sue Forster in her book) is to stop the silence, call the bullying out and report it where you feel you can. You are not likely to be the only person affected by that bully. A practised bully will have many victims. Try to find some support from other victims, mentors or through assertiveness training and counselling. Unfortunately, bullying will be a constant throughout your career, and you will need these skills often. Also, watch out for others who have been or are being bullied. Make sure you offer support to the victims of bullying and never become a bully yourself.

Important life lessons

People often ask me how I can work in such a sad field and whether it affects me too much on an emotional level. I always reply that I enjoy my work and find it a privilege to help people during the most challenging period in their lives. Today, many more people with cancer survive than they did when I started cancer nursing, so the outlook has improved. Of course, there are still many people who die every day from cancer. I aim to try to make that time filled with as much quality as possible. I can do that by providing care and compassion whilst caring for them when they come to the hospital to have their chemotherapy. I teach them how to manage their side effects to ensure they still have an acceptable quality of life whilst having their treatment. I can advocate for them within the health system when necessary. Together with my nursing colleagues, I can help to provide a pleasant and friendly environment for them to come to when having their treatment.

I think you will surprise yourself that you have decided on a career in cancer nursing. I don't think you would have anticipated working with many people who will not survive their illness. But you will find that this is precisely what you are comfortable doing. With quality role-modelling from others who possess more experience than you, you will find you have the right nature for this role. You have some natural skills in communicating with others and can learn from others to develop skills for those more difficult conversations you will need to have with people about death and dying. You will also learn the ability to turn off your thoughts from your workday by rekindling your love of horse riding. Having this hobby will help you let go of your day as you head straight to the horses to ride and care for them.

One of the most important lessons you will learn is that life can be short. Not everybody gets to live the entire length of life that most of us expect. Caring for people of your own age and younger who are dying will make this much more real to you. You will learn some vital lessons so early in your life such as: the importance of living every day as full as possible, not taking life and others for granted and truly appreciating what we do have, especially our family and friends.

Always remember the valuable friendships you have developed over your years in nursing. Your colleagues and your patients are the ones that make your everyday a lovely experience. To have the chance to meet these people and develop relationships with them is a great privilege. Remember the nurses, doctors and patients who have taught you valuable life lessons. Take the time to pass on those lessons and provide a great learning and positive environment for others to work.

Always remain patient and compassionate with your patients to provide them with the highest quality nursing care possible.

Summary of advice for new nurses

- Nursing is about caring for patients. Good communication and compassion are two of the most useful skills you can bring to work every day

- There are many specialities to choose in nursing. If you have the opportunity, explore some specialties you haven't seen when you were a student

- Bullying is a reality in nursing and almost every workforce today. To survive, you need to develop some resilience and assertiveness skills

- If you see someone else being bullied, help them to call it out if you can, and support that bullied person afterwards

- Don't ever participate in bullying yourself or enable it to happen to others

- Once you have qualified, this is just the start of your career and learning experience. Approach your career with a life-long learning approach to keep up with the changes you will see in your lifetime

- Commit yourself to helping other new nurses as they enter their career. Educating and mentoring is extremely important in developing nurses' skills and knowledge

- Nursing can be stressful no matter where you work, so take time to debrief with your colleagues when you can

- And finally, enjoy putting your heart and soul into your career as it can be extremely rewarding

About Jackie:

Jackie is a registered nurse who completed her hospital-based nursing training in 1985 at Gold Coast Hospital, Queensland. She found her passion for cancer nursing early in her career after completing a post-graduate certificate in Oncology Nursing at the Royal Brisbane Hospital in 1987. Together with Medical Oncologist Dr Robert Hitchins, Jackie was fundamental in the planning, development and ongoing management of the first chemotherapy day unit on the Gold Coast in 1989. Together they forged a path to enable patients to have chemotherapy on the Gold Coast for the first time instead of having to travel one hour to Brisbane for treatments, appointments and investigations.

In 1989, Jackie was a finalist in the Queenslander of the Year Award, and in 1996, Jackie was selected to represent Australia to speak on Health and Education in the Asia Pacific Youth Programme held in Japan. Jackie has held the positions of Clinical Nurse Consultant, Nurse Manager and Nurse Educator in public and private hospitals. She has worked for Cancer Council Queensland supporting patients on the Gold Coast and their state-wide Helpline and been a regular speaker at cancer support group meetings.

Jackie is also committed to educating and training nurses new to cancer care, and will complete her Master of Nursing Education in early 2022. Jackie's passion for cancer nursing and her caring nature has impacted many nurses, patients and their loved ones over four decades.

You can contact Jackie at: morganjackie@me.com

Afterward

Judy Lonergan

Knowledge is power, and for nurses that comes with education and reflection, and there is arguably no more important nursing endeavour than to learn.

Back in the late sixties when I entered nursing as a Cadet Nurse, the education I received consisted of two weeks of lectures in a classroom with some practical education in a ward. Was it any wonder that we blew up the steriliser when we put 30 mercury-filled glass thermometers in the 'bomb' to sterilise them? Then we had to reimburse the hospital for the cost of the thermometers out of our pay.

The educator was up the front of the classroom using a blackboard and chalk. Then, in the '70s, when I commenced my three-year nursing registration training there were block lectures after which I commenced on an orthopaedic ward where I followed the second or third year nurses who taught me many things, such as how to care for and monitor intravenous infusions by counting the drips of the fluid without relying on a machine. On night shifts there would be two of us for 30 to 40 patients. We had a procedure book in which procedures were signed off by three people. In order to improve patient outcomes, education is paramount. During this time, I learned from my senior nurses and whilst on night shifts I was shown how to monitor intravenous infusions. Learning the basics is still very important. Nursing at ground level prepares a nurse to be a good carer, but it doesn't prepare one to enter the research discipline, a managing role or an educator role. Nowadays, student nurses are preceptered, ideally with a one-on-one approach, but when there are no staff, it can be a one-to-four ratio.

Education has evolved over the last 40 years from the block lectures to white boards to technology, where procedures could be filmed, digitalised, analysed and changes made for the best patient outcomes. Collaborative quality education through hands-on tertiary and university mediums makes a significant impact on health care outcomes. It is important that the nursing workforce is appropriately educated and supported in developing the skills and confidence to support and safely care for their patients. Highly educated nurses can also now be involved in decision-making about future trends in treatments, patient care and disease prevention strategies.

Technology has allowed nurses to network and connect with likeminded colleagues around the world, as well as provide a broader scope of education. Reflecting upon one's nursing career is another educational tool as the authors have done in their chapters in this book.

Wendy Trevarthen

Nursing is a journey from the unfamiliar to the familiar in a cyclic pattern as you move through your career, building resilience through these changes and developing skills to enhance your workplace wellbeing along the way. Having strategies to maintain this wellbeing is essential for longevity in this role, and one aspect of self-care that I have often denied for myself and have seen lacking in others. We are born givers, empaths ready to 'sacrifice' ourselves and our own priorities for the welfare of our patients. Being aware of our triggers for the many emotions that we endure on the job is vital to building a tool kit to circumvent any negative outcomes from the day-to-day work that we endure. Building your toolkit for self-care is not indulgent.

Over these authors' careers there have been dramatic changes in the way in which we have been taught our profession, with most of us working with colleagues who were not 'cut out to be a nurse' and who were able to recognise this within the first three months of training, compared to today's registered nurses (RNs) who spend a good four years investing their interest into a profession that may not be their first choice. How lucky were the nurses in 'our day' were to be able to change their mind after just three months and move into a career pathway that fulfilled their souls. Those that stayed for 12 months also had the opportunity to register as an enrolled nurse (EN), recognising that this was a better option for their personal skill set.

We all endured some part of our career supporting for greater conditions in our awards. For me this included striking during 1988 for better conditions such as our 10-hour breaks, longer annual leave for the shift work, and for those day workers, an ADO once every four weeks. This greatly enhanced our ability to manage fatigue issues. I think this battle has been forgotten a little, with the creep of entitlements being taken for granted and even eroded – again for the lack of acknowledgement of self-care and the long-term health effects of doing the profession that we love for our entire working life.

Nursing exposes us to many situations and provides us with many lessons to be learned along the way. As the most trusted profession, we need to build avenues where we can continue to trust amongst our own circles too, to enable us to work through situations. Mentoring is a model that works well amongst other health professionals,

Afterward

and you are encouraged to select mentors who have your best interest at heart. What about coaching ourselves? We are all trained in the art of coaching our clients with their goals, but how do we coach each other to achieve ours? It is astonishing that the average age of our RNs is rapidly increasing and is currently at 44 years of age[xi]. This indicates that there is a lot of work to do to support our nurses within the workforce, recognising their experience and wisdom and trying to keep them in the profession that they love.

For those of you who are just starting out in your nursing career, heed the wise words within this book, acknowledge your nursing ancestry and the hard work that has gone before you and do your research on your entitlements that should not be taken for granted. Continue to be curious, learn from each other and seek positive circles in which you can flourish.

References

Chapter 1

[i] https://languages.oup.com/google-dictionary-en/

[ii] Canning, D., Rosenberg, J. P., & Yates, P. (2007). Therapeutic relationships in specialist palliative care nursing practice. *International Journal of Palliative Nursing, 13*(5), 222-229.

[iii] https://charterforcompassion.org/charter/affirm

[iv] Kellehear, A. (1999). *Health promoting palliative care.* Oxford University Press.

[v] https://www.phpci.org/

[vi] Rosenberg, J. (2011). Whose business is dying? Death, the home and palliative care. *Cultural Studies Review, 17*(1), 15-30.

[vii] Rilke, R. M., & Burnham, J. M. (1993). Letters to a Young Poet. 1934. *Trans. MD Herter Norton.* New York: WW Norton & Co.

[viii] Kain, L., & Kain, S. (2009). *The Little Brown Book: Mary MacKillop's spirituality in our everyday lives.* St Pauls.

Chapter 5

[ix] Australian Nursing and Midwifery Federation. (2021). *Bullying in the workplace.* http://anmf.org.au/documents/policies/P_Bullying_in_the_workplace.pdf

Chapter 6

[x] Forster, S. (2011). *Do you want bullying with that?: Bullying across the age continuum.* eBook Partnership.

Afterward

[xi] Australian Institute of Health and Welfare. (2016). *Nursing and midwifery workforce 2015. https://www.aihw.gov.au/reports/workforce/ nursing-and-midwifery-workforce-2015/contents/who-are-nurses-and-midwives*

www.ingramcontent.com/pod-product-compliance
Lightning Source LLC
Chambersburg PA
CBHW021147080526
44588CB00008B/247